Praise for **Questions from Dad**

Questions From Dad *is truly outstanding. I highly recommend Dwight's method as a very effective way to develop better relationships between children and their parents. Communicating through the tests described in this book should be a win-win situation for all. P.S. The drawings are terrific!*

David L. Levy, Esq., National President
Children's Rights Council, Washington D.C.

We all know someone who wants to have a better relationship with their child . . . **Questions From Dad** *provides a healthy alternative to worrying and feeling helpless while trying to establish or maintain that relationship. Parents who see their children daily could learn a lot about parenting through this book as well!*

Travis Ballard, Esq., President
National Congress for Men and Children, Washington D.C.

This book can help many people—not only absentee fathers. Whether their separation be due to a break in the family unit, traveling for business, being in the armed forces or in prison, **Questions From Dad** *shows absent parents how they can stay in touch with their children.*

Michael Bowers, M.A., Executive Director
American Association for Marriage and Family Therapy,
Washington D. C.

An innovative approach to encouraging a long distance parent-child relationship, one that any parent and child living apart from one another would find fun and rewarding.

Jennifer Isham, National President
Mothers Without Custody, Houston, Texas

Questions From Dad *is a metaphor for love from dad, and Twilley's method of loving his daughter can inspire within any father that spark of creativity, caring and playfulness that will leave both him and his child with a legacy of love.*

Warren Farrell, Ph.D., Author
The Myth of Male Power, and *Why Men Are the Way They Are*

Questions From Dad *can help turn shallow conversations and awkward silences into productive discussions between parents and children. We commend this book as a unique how-to manual on maintaining and improving communication with children.*

Dick Woods, Accredited Access Counselor and Director
Fathers for Equal Rights, Inc. and Iowa Access Enforcement Project,
Des Moines

Within ten minutes of finishing the book, my first <u>Grammie Wants to Know</u> was started. I now have a fun and creative way to communicate with my grandchildren, who live three thousand miles away. Thank you from the bottom of my heart.

Sheila Sands, State Coordinator
Chidren's Rights Council of Massachusetts, Springfield, Massachusetts

*It is our experience that, with the changing economic climate and the concomitant strain it puts on the traditional family, parents, in many cases, do not know how to communciate with their children. **Questions From Dad** provides a safe, easy and effective vehicle for establishing the vital links that must exist between parent and child.*

Dennis Brown, Ph.D., Executive Director
The National Institute for Child Custody and Divorce Awareness, Inc.,
Lincoln Park, New Jersey

*Fathers today need all the help they can get in order to effectively communicate with their children. **Questions From Dad** plays an important role in fulfilling that need. Perhaps the greatest endorsement for the Dad's Tests comes from my six-year-old daughter, who often climbs up in my lap and asks me to read Mr. Twilley's questionnaires to her.*

Charles A. Ballard, Founder/President
National Institute for Responsible Fatherhood & Family Development,
Cleveland, Ohio

This book literally places the children first, by enhancing their ability to know their parents through creative communication. Thank you for sharing this marvelous method with the parents and children who so desperately need to know each other.

George and Lesley Wimberely, Director and President
National Association of State VOCAL Organizations,
Orangevale, California

***Questions From Dad** offers an exciting solution to the long-distance communications problem that is plaguing more and more families, and families separated by a marital breakup are but a small part of the individuals that can use this book. It is a must-read for all parents who find themselves periodically physically separated from their children.*

Ray Hart, State Association President
Fathers Rights Association of New York State, Inc., Rochester, New York

*Any suggested means of communication between an absent parent and child, whether the distance be long or short, is a welcome addition in attempting to build a bridge between parental responsibility and child well-being. **Questions From Dad** achieves this status, in what may indeed be called a unique manner.*

James I. Taylor, Past President and Legislative Liaison
Equal Rights for Fathers of New York State, Clinton, New York

Questions

from

DAD

Dedicated to the best dad,
George William Twilley
(1926-1984)

And to the memory of my earliest partner in song, Phil Seymour,
and these greatly missed friends:
Annie, Mollie-Twilley, Mollie, Ozzie, Dixie the Duck,
Beethoven and Beethoven, Jr., Mel, Kee-Kee and Lester.

Questions *from* DAD

A Very Cool Way to Communicate with Kids

By Dwight Twilley

Edited by Joe Klein

Introduction by Dr. Susan Forward, Ph.D.

CHARLES E. TUTTLE COMPANY, INC
BOSTON · RUTLAND, VERMONT · TOKYO

In conjunction with reading this book, know your legal rights and obligations as they pertain to your relationships with your children. As much as the author would like to see as many readers as possible utilizing the technique described in this book to improve communication with their children, he is in no way encouraging any parent to disobey any court order or statute.

Published in 1994 by

CHARLES E. TUTTLE COMPANY, INC
of Boston, Rutland, Vermont, and Tokyo
with editorial offices at
153 Milk Street, 5th Floor
Boston, Massachusetts 02109

ISBN 0-8048-1984-X

LIBRARY OF CONGRESS CATALOG CARD NUMBER 94-60040

COVER AND TEXT DESIGN BY JILL WINITZER

2 4 6 8 9 7 5 3 1

PRINTED IN THE UNITED STATES OF AMERICA

CONTENTS

> " A very cool way to communicate with kids. "

ACKNOWLEDGMENTS

T he author would like to acknowledge the contributions and inspiration from the following people, who truly helped make this book possible.

First, my daughter Dion, because she's the best that any dad could ask for. Next, my editor, advisor and friend, Joe Klein, who saw the first "Dad's Tests" and convinced me to write this book, and saw us through the process without sustaining serious injuries! Then there's Jan Allison Rose for her love and support through endless nights of rewrites, for the use of Allison Entertainment Inc.'s office and computer system and for feeding Mow and Coco when I went off to live at Kinko's. Dion's mother, Linda, for allowing me to keep the lines of communication open and for obviously being a great mom. And, of course, my own mom, Alberta Twilley, for bawling out the parents of the kid who beaned me on the head with a rock!

The assistance of the following friends and supporters is also greatly appreciated. Jerry McCulley for his dogged encouragement, Rocky Burnette for his dadly rock and roll wisdom, ZOX for his ultra-pop visionary eye, Ciaran MacGowan for his Irish lensmanship, Robert Knight for the shot with shades, Morey Klein, Sue Rose, Wendy Gardner Moore and her sensible photocopy machine, Carrie R. Hyde, Susan, Peter and Miranda

Holsapple, speech-man Jeff Cooper, computer-dude Fast Eddie Maurer, computer-pilot Fred Blechman, agents B. J. Robbins and Ken Sherman, Dr. Susan Forward, Ph.D., Don Menn, Dr. Carole Lieberman, M.D., Phil Lobel and Lobeline Communications, Bill Holdship and BAM Magazine, Karen Glauber at HITS, Ken Barnes of Radio and Records, Tom Lanham, Bruce Grakal, Esq., Dan Bourgoise, Bud Scoppa, Karen Momme, David Levy, Esq., Dick Woods, Russell Fish, Sonny Burmeister, Helen Grieco, Steve "K-Man" Kamer, Santos "H.D." Flaniken and Rock-A-Bear, Jeffery R. Leving, Esq., Gil Savage, Wayne & Garth, and who could forget the agony and ecstasy bestowed upon us by nearly every Kinko's Copies store in the San Fernando Valley of L.A. and Santa Monica!

Thanks to all the people at our publishing company: Peter Ackroyd, Roberta Scimone, Kathryn Sky-Peck for her editorial endeavors, Lorrie Andonian and her pub-licity-minded mind, Mike Kerber, and a special thanks to Jim McMullan for introducing us to the Tuttles. Finally, to all the pets and characters, who give us so much to talk about. Mow, Coco, Carrie, Yodeler, Auhee, Toby, Princess, Mohawk, Buddy, Geoffry, Dixie the Parakeet, Tweety, Julio Mangles, Mr. Rat, Max-Dog, Mario, The Flea and Snake Families, The Little Man In Chinatown and all the new personalities yet to come!

INTRODUCTION

by Dr. Susan Forward, Ph.D.

Half of all marriages end in divorce. Each year, over 1.2 million promises of "til death do us part" get broken and millions of adults begin the process of healing.

But what of the children? They too need to heal, and though mom and dad no longer want to spend their lives together, the children didn't make that choice. They still need to feel connected to and loved by both parents. They need to know that the end of love between mom and dad does not mean the end of love between them and mom or dad. Unfortunately, divorce in a family with children results in the physical separation of the children from one of the parents—most commonly the father. So the child, who has already experienced the loss of family life as he or she knew it, now experiences another loss—daddy doesn't live here anymore.

In the fast-paced world in which we live, staying connected to our children, and in touch with their needs, likes and dislikes, dreams and wishes, is difficult enough—even when we live under the same roof. How, then, can a dad be anything other than just a friendly

"If you're looking for ways to connect with your child, you've come to the right place."

acquaintance if he lives far away? Or if he only visits weekly or monthly?

Through *Questions from Dad.*

Dwight Twilley has done something quite remarkable. Not only has he maintained open communication with his thirteen-year old daughter Dionne, whom he has never lived with, but he has found a way to be present for her as a parent despite his physical absence.

I don't think Dwight ever realized, when he put his first Dad's Test in the mailbox years ago, that he had engineered a bridge for estranged parents and children to stay in touch, to keep love alive. That he had come up with an anchor to keep the parent-child relationship from drifting and ultimately getting lost.

Dwight's physical distance is easier to bear because of that bridge and that anchor. His Dad's Tests maintain a constant dialogue between him and his daughter. And they are *fun*— fun for Dwight to draft, fun for Dionne to get, fun for her to fill in, fun for him to get back! These tests have enabled Dwight and Dionne to know each other in ways that some children and parents who live together never do.

Dionne told me, "The questions let me know that dad was interested in things I never thought he'd be interested in— like my cat." There may be an

Dionne (age 11) with Bud and Toby. Photo by Linda Twilley

entire trove of special details about your child that *Questions from Dad* could dig up for you!

And I can't help believing that these tests also have allowed Dwight to get in touch with the kid inside him. He has reached way inside himself to find questions that are funny, puzzles and drawings and bits of silliness. To work, the tests need to focus the attention on the child, so Dwight needed to think of things Dionne might like and respond to. As Dionne grew and matured, so did the tests, leaving Dwight with insight into his daughter at age ten, eleven, twelve . . .

The effort Dwight put forth to communicate with Dionne is rare and very special—and thus has rewarded him with a relationship with his daughter that is similarly rare and very special.

How many fathers out there see their children once in a while as part of their custody arrangement? How many of you send presents in the mail in the hope of being remembered? How many of you go home at the end of the trip to the zoo or the mall or the baseball game with a sinking feeling in your hearts and stomachs that you don't know that little person anymore? That you have little in common, that you have nothing to say to each other, nothing to share?

If you're looking for ways to connect with your child, you've come to the right place. You can't maintain a parenting role based on "once in a while." Your own set of *Questions from Dad* can become your link to your child, your private haven, your "home" together. Once you try this book's approach, you'll wonder how you (and your child) ever did without it!

I spoke to Dionne about her dad's tests. She clearly has benefited from them. She is blossoming into adolescence with the security and self-assurance that comes from feeling accepted and loved. That is

> **"**
> How many
> of you send
> presents
> in the mail
> in the hope
> of being
> remembered?
> **"**

> **Unlike a conversation, your tests will stick around.**

to both of her parents' credit. Dwight and his ex-wife Linda were able to separate from each other and still share the parenting of Dionne. The purity of Dwight's tests had a lot to do with that. He never used the tests as an investigative look into his ex-wife's life, or as a way to weasel his way back into it, or to bad-mouth anybody, or to twist truths, or in any way threaten or undermine Linda's role as primary care-giver. I cannot stress the importance of this enough. The *Questions from Dad* method which Dwight Twilley has devised is a wonderful—even magical—form of communication for parents and kids. But it is also sacrosanct. To work its magic, its unwritten rules need to be honored.

Dionne feels close to her dad. She feels comfortable sharing silly stories and drawings with him, knowing he will guard their little secrets. She feels understood. She feels loved. I wondered if she didn't sometimes feel like the tests were a chore. "It's a lot of questions," I probed. "Yes, but I look forward to getting them!" Dionne said. The most profound impact of Dwight's tests was revealed to me when Dionne told me: "The tests make it easier for me to talk to my dad when I finally get to see him. Because we're already friends."

Children often walk away from divorce not only wounded, but feeling guilty and somehow responsible for the break-up. It is important to let children know—in no uncertain terms—that the divorce was not their fault. Emotional wounds can scar children forever. The best way to help children heal is to maintain a constant, supportive world for them in which they feel cared for and loved. And the most loving thing we can do for them is to show them we genuinely care about their thoughts and feelings. Their future happiness, and their capacity to love others and be loved depends on the supportive foundation you establish for them. The building blocks for that foundation are the thoughts and experiences you share, the little things that make you laugh together, the stories you quietly tell each other when no one else is listening.

You'll find you will grow as an individual through this process. Writing allows us the luxury of forethought and editing in a way that talking does not. Unlike a conversation, your tests will stick around, a tangible history of your communication with your child. The beauty of the permanence of the written word is often lost in a world of sound-bytes and MTV. Time will pass, and you and your child will find yourselves looking back at the tests over and over again. They will make you remember. They will make you laugh. They may even make you cry.

Children don't have the same language skills as adults. You will need to take special care to make your tests age-appropriate. Children can't always find words for what they want to say. Dwight's varied question styles provide possibilities and choices for kids who could otherwise not express themselves. Mixing in humorous question-and-answer choices reinforces the notion that this is more a game than a "test."

Keep your own child's interests in mind. If she is a budding sleuth, come up with a hidden clues mystery game. If he loves animals, cut up pictures from magazines and decorate your test with them. Dwight is great at this. He mixes funny tales with games, crossword puzzles, doodles, and other things to keep Dionne interested and connected. Remember, the process is supposed to be *fun*! Have fun with it.

You will find that you can gain deep insight into your child by the answers to his or her tests. You can also give your child deep insight into what you value

> **"**
> The tests make it easier for me to talk to my dad when I finally get to see him, because we're already friends.
> **"**

and believe. Think about it. What do you want to pass on to your daughter or son? What do you want him or her to know about you? How do you want to be remembered?

Dwight mixed serious questions and issues into the fun ones, thus making the serious ones more "invisible" and more likely to get an answer. Point-blank questions about boys, drugs, or grades could be deemed too direct and make your child recoil rather than respond. Be prepared to give serious responses serious consideration, however. If your child's test reveals something you are concerned about, talk about it. Don't just enjoy the cute, funny and light-hearted nature of these tests. Delve into the depth of feeling which some answers may disclose—and use that as a springboard for a heart-to-heart talk! The tests are not meant to replace—or be an easy way out of—visits, phone calls, letters and cards.

What the Dad's Tests gave Dwight was insight into how to be a better parent to Dionne, a way to stay tuned into his little girl's life as the weeks and months went by.

What the Dad's Tests gave Dionne was love. Revealing himself through humor, puzzles and little games, Dwight showed Dionne that he had learned from her previous answers and was responsive to them. She felt connected to her dad through these tests as few children ever do.

Far more than being just fun tests, the *Questions from Dad* turned Dwight and Dionne into secret pen-pals. Through the tests, Dwight and Dionne were able to bond on many different levels. They shared stories, inside jokes, and little bits of themselves. That way, when they did get to see each other, Dwight and Dionne

"

Questions from Dad will act as a key to the wonders of childhood—it will be a touching journey for both of you.

"

had as much (or more) in common as any parent and child
who live together. They were
friends.

Questions from Dad will
act as a key to the wonders of
childhood. It will be a touching
journey for both of you. It will
alter and affect you in ways you
cannot now imagine. Open your
heart wide. And let your child in!

"Bodey Don't
Mind," by Dwight

PART 1

HOW AND WHY

CALLING
ALL DADS

It is not the purpose of this book to address any of the nagging emotional issues such as custody battles, child support and legal disputes that so often hang like ugly clouds over families separated.

What I am trying to do is rally "long distance dads" and, for that matter, all parents behind the idea of increasing the amount and quality of communication with their kids. Whether you're mere blocks or thousands of miles from your child, the term "long distance" could apply to you if the dialogue between you and your child is limited, strained or inadequate.

That distance now separating so many children from their parents is the simple reason I emphasize the need for this exclusive dialogue. If, like me, you have found phone calls and letters lacking substance and falling short of asserting your presence in your child's life, relief is at hand!

In this book, I will present a unique and effective method which has allowed me to establish a productive and unprecedented line of communication with my child. For me, the positive nature of this simple procedure has shattered the distance barrier—forever.

Later, in more detail, I will describe this system that

> **"** You've got a lot to say—and there's much to discover ahead. **"**

my daughter and I now commonly refer to as the "Dad's Test." Call it whatever you like, but this intimate and fun questionnaire from dad is, at once, a means of communication, a source of camaraderie, and a sure-fire way to solicit answers to any question a long distance dad—or any parent—could ponder.

I know that, while some dads enjoy calm waters, others, sometimes by virtue of their own mistakes, experience the more nightmarish side of broken marriages.

It is my hope that, even in the worst cases, the Dad's Test might slide through and bridge the gap between the bitterness of a bad dilemma and what is best for a child.

It is not my intention to instigate finger pointing between the sexes. And, while I will be harping on about how the tests should be just between you and your child, this doesn't imply that they should be used as weapons aimed to alienate others or further disrupt already shaken ground. These questionnaires, as personal in nature as they are, should not become ammunition between you and your ex-spouse. Keep the "grown up" issues away from your quizzes! The Dad's Tests should be thought of as "magic dry cleaners," designed to "shrink miles" instead of shirts.

Naturally, whenever possible, amiable communication with your ex-spouse or the custodial guardian can reduce stress on your child and make your well-intended test more welcome as it passes through a potentially enemy household.

This test, which only demonstrates love and con-

Dionne's drawing of Dad.

cern for a person whom it took two people to create, may in itself plant a seed of reconciliation.

I also want to acknowledge that some dads secure custody of their children, and I'm sure that the "Mom's Test" would be equally welcome to a single-parent child.

As I am a dad, I'm not really equipped to address the nuances of the "Mom's slant," but the concept remains the same. Step-parents, grandparents, and separated siblings are also nominee quiz-creators. Some of you who have business that keeps you away from home or who are in the military may be candidates too. Even you guys behind bars could simulate your presence through the tests.What a constructive and rewarding way to pass the time!

Those of you who devote too much time to your careers might even discover a welcome recipient of the Dad's Test in your own home. Kids are always excited to find something in the mail for them. What a surprise to receive a test from Dad's work address! Slipped under the pillow, your quiz could be serious tooth-fairy competition. It's hard communicating with a teenager who has locked herself in her room. Fortunately, a Dad's Test will slide under the door. (My daughter has just reached her teens, and I'm already beginning to see shades of some of the unsettling "coming attractions.") We all hesitate to admit that we eventually have to let 'em go. But I'm counting on the Dad's Tests to keep my foot in the door as long as possible.

Dionne's Halloween

Let's face it. It's no cake walk for a distant dad. It's not easy to jump start communication that has run down—or even died—over a period of time. Rather than look for solutions, it may seem easier just to blame yourself, someone else, or run away from the problem altogether. The resulting void can leave you feeling even more guilty or ashamed. You may feel uncomfortable about the way you are perceived by others, or even think of yourself as a dysfunctional dad. Taking the "hopeless hat" off can be tough. I know. I've worn that puppy for months at a time. But, after the much needed gloom and despair and sufficient time spent cursing the sky, it's time to start thinking about another hat—the hat that you are denying your child. What would you rather see above your

Dionne's great-grandfather.

•••••••••▶

kid's head—a question mark, or a crown that reads, "You can say what you want about my dad, but I know he cares about me!"

A dad who feels angry or helpless can elevate his self-esteem when he discovers that just a few hours of his time can have such a profound and positive effect on his child. A release from the discouragement of believing that there are no options could be at all of our fingertips through the Dad's Tests!

It's no secret that we dads are capable of torturing ourselves, receiving great torture and torturing others. Perhaps, now, we can take a breath and look at more redeeming horizons! You're not reading this book because you like the clever way I turn a phrase. You love your kid. Most of you were not just reckless drivers who crashed into parenthood; it was your dream. Others who swore never to have a child discovered they were more than eager to put away the power tools or switch off a football game to search for Barbie's lost slipper.

It doesn't take much more than the first time a tiny hand wraps around your finger for you to know that your child is both the future—and the past.

When you look at your child's face or study a photo, you may also see your mother, your grandfather and even unfamiliar faces that carry the wisdom of ancestors spiraling back through history. With this, it becomes clear that the importance of passing on the things you believe in to your child is equalled by how much you can learn.

You've got a lot to say—and there's much to discover ahead. It's never too late for anything that might help you bond with your child.

I'm calling on all dads to sharpen pencils, dust off typewriters, power up computers and do whatever is necessary to begin their first tests!

> **"**
> You can say what you want about my dad, but I know he cares about me!
> **"**

I'm hoping that this book will succeed in eliminating excuses—and inspire communication. The next time you hear one of your friends ragging on about the distance between he and his child, tell him about the tests and show him some of yours. Then, tell him to shut up and sharpen his pencil!

THE ROAD
TO THE TESTS

T oday, so much energy is centered on the problems and affairs of us grown-ups that our children often become a secondary issue. My primary mission in writing this book is to advance the idea of the "Dad's Test"—and putting our children first. I'm not writing this book to tell you how or why I came to be a long-distance dad. It's not my intent to focus on the soap-opera aspects of broken relationships—mine included. This book isn't about divorce—I'm sure my story could be topped by almost anyone you bump into on the street. But a little background will help provide a thumb-nail sketch of the road that—for better or worse—led to the Dad's Tests.

Shortly after I graduated high school, I met a girl named Linda. We maintained a steady relationship for years, and eventually got married in our early twenties. At the time, I was still a struggling musician, knocking around the clubs in Tulsa, Oklahoma. I begrudgingly found part-time jobs to support my emerging career. The short trips I made to Memphis and Nashville for recording didn't have a significant effect on our lives. But I knew I was reaching the point where, to fulfill my

> **"**
> Dad!
> send more
> tests!
> **"**

musical ambitions, I would need to commit to a more substantial journey—this time to the west coast.

Eventually, with the reluctant approval of Linda, plans for this "business trip" of undetermined length were in motion. Complete with band, bags, guitars and a rusted Olds, I was finally on my way to L.A., where I was sure success in the music business was waiting. Inevitably, like a thousand other wide-eyed kids, I found myself on the streets of Hollywood with a demo tape in my pocket. I was prepared to struggle and rough it out for as long as the few hundred bucks I had in my pocket would allow me to scrape by. It seemed like a worthwhile sacrifice for the chance to be discovered. Ironically, the struggle only amounted to a couple of weeks and a lot of cheap frozen dinners. In a strange

"Ice Captain," by Dwight

quirk of fate, I was offered a recording contract from Shelter Records, whose home office was in Tulsa. How bizarre! After traveling over a thousand miles, I would be signing with a label located only a few miles from my house!

Not so many months later, I had a hit record called "I'm On Fire." Linda joined me in Los Angeles. Over the next few years, I was recording, doing concert tours, television shows and getting a little lost in the show-biz fast lane. The money and celebrity were great, but there were prices to pay.

I was like a kid in a rocket ship—things were changing so fast and drastically. The first casualty was my marriage. I guess when you don't know what planet you're on, it's hard to be on someone else's.

Linda decided to move back to Tulsa. Then, the traumatic and emotionally-charged dilemma of our separation became almost surrealistic when fate stepped in and added another, even more sobering, factor to the equation: We were going to have a child.

Linda and I had drifted too far apart for a realistic chance at reconciliation, and, in the interim, I had met another woman that I was beginning to think seriously about. In spite of all this, there was never any question in Linda's mind about having the baby. It was her choice to make, and I supported her decision.

Looking back, as much as I would like to blame the failure of my marriage on all the things that were happening to me and the amount of time I was having to spend on my career, I must admit that I was just too young and irresponsible for a commitment as grown up as marriage. Likewise, I was miles away from even thinking about parenthood.

With time, the separation seemed reasonably amicable, and I think we both felt comfortable about getting on with our lives. There had been a lot of love

"Eggplant Baby"
photo by Linda Twilley

between us for many years. Perhaps this child was meant to be the consummation of all that had been good. Linda and I recently agreed that we did it all backwards. Most people get married and have a baby. We had a baby and got divorced!

The next seven or eight months seemed like seven or eight minutes. I was in the middle of recording when I received the long distance call. A baby girl was born, and I was her father. I had been raised in a family with four brothers and no sisters. The idea that somewhere in the world there was a tiny, bald-headed female creature that might look a little like me was a mind-twisting concept.

The night she was born, I thought it was agreed that her name would be "Dion," spelled D-I-O-N. I didn't like the traditional female spelling. But somehow, it was "Dionne" that finally appeared on the birth certificate. Perhaps that was the first indication of what being a long distance dad would be like. I spell her name D-I-O-N to this day, but not for any negative reasons. I like it that when Dionne sees "Dion," she knows that dad's involved, and I kind of get a kick out of thinking it might allow her her own little alter-ego.

No absent dad can ever forget the day he receives the first photos of his child. After the required time spent confirming that ears and eyes were in their proper locations, my first impression was, "She looks like

an eggplant!" I went around for the next few days calling her "Eggplant Baby." As the weeks passed, I began
to receive more photos. Soon I was forced to ask
myself the question, "Am I prejudiced, or is she possibly the most beautiful child ever to grace a Polaroid?"

My recording schedule had not allowed me to visit
my new-born child. I began to experience a new and
uneasy feeling. Something was wrong. There was a little more than a thousand miles between the person I
had been—and my new identity as a dad. It was a
strange sensation to miss someone I'd never met.

Then, at a time when I thought things couldn't get
any more complicated or confusing, I became entan-
gled in a show business tradition
I neither expected, nor was prepared for. There was a legal dis-
pute involving my recording
contract. Everything came to an
abrupt stop. I had complete con-
fidence in myself as an artist, but
it began to become apparent that
I didn't have a clue about con-
ducting business. Truckloads of
money seemed to be ending up—
in other people's trucks.

> Daddy spells it Dion
>
> Mommy spells it Dionne
>
> Ozzie says meowon
>
> Molly sings the same song
>
> Auhee, Molly and Susan three
>
> Spell it with a mark ♥
>
> But Toby never learned to read
>
> He spells it with a bark!

With the financial strain and
endless legal procedures, it was
impossible for me to leave L.A.—and, more and more
difficult to think of myself as a responsible adult—let
alone a father. I felt helpless.

So, as a result of events that were out of my hands
and problems I most likely brought upon myself, I was
forced to sit by and watch month after month pass,
while my daughter, so far away, was growing inch by
inch, never knowing her father.

After a virtual cake-walk of lawyers, the legal hassles finally were resolved. I ended up at a new record company, EMI, and I was glad to finally be back in the studio working on a new album. That album, "Scuba Divers," would include a new song called "Dion Baby."

Now that things were back on track and "Mr. Wallet" was much happier, a release from this nagging, innate sensation of incompleteness seemed within reach! I was beginning to realize that the most important creation of my life might now just be a plane ticket away. Things had gone well in the studio, and the sessions were coming to an end. At last—the time had arrived to meet my daughter.

Just before making the trek back home to Tulsa, I felt a great sense of relief. Since Dion was born, I had felt guilty thinking that Linda may not have really understood what I had been going through, and perhaps misread my absence to mean that I didn't care about my kid. But once I told her I was coming home to see Dion, I felt she, too, was relieved to know that, although we had separated, I really did want to be a part of my daughter's life.

"Music," by Dwight

I was nervous when I arrived at the house. I really didn't know what to expect. I knocked, and, after a few long moments, two tiny hands emerged, tugging at the door. And there she was.

It was questionable whether or not I had ever really found true love in my life. But it became immediately obvious that I had been hopelessly seduced by a squirming angel, barely a year old, who loved to stretch my face and poke her fingers in my eyeballs and nose.

I remember, like a bozo, I paraded my kid around Tulsa, showing her off to friends, family and people who could care less! This "dad thing" wasn't such a bad deal after all. Before, it seemed like the only thing I was ever really excited about was my "new record." Now, I had my "new kid!" When I finally had to return to L.A., I knew that I would never be the same person. I had become . . . a dad.

At that moment, it finally struck me that, while Linda had always wanted a child (and I figured that eventually it might happen), I never really appreciated or understood the whole parenthood picture. I didn't grow up holding a baby doll in my arms. Instead, I was armed with toy guns, monster models and, later, guitars. When I was five years old, no one said "Dwight, would you like a little baby?" On "Father Knows Best" and "Leave It To Beaver," the dad was just there and the kids were already there. *What would Ward Cleaver have done in my situation?* I was raised at a time when boys were somewhat oblivious to the baby thing. Someone else did that! I wonder if it would be a healthier world today if little girls would have occasionally been faced with the task of gluing together Frankenstein and little boys were encouraged to learn to change Baby Big Tear's diaper.

Anyway, over the next few years, I was able to maintain a fair amount of contact with Dion. There were occasional visits and phone calls, and I'd send her postcards from across the country

ディオン・ベイビー

DION BABY

Dion you make me
Better when I was crazy
Well April it was rain it was hazy
But you were my only baby

Dion baby, oh, oh, oh, Dion baby
Well I wanna be with you
I want to be with you
I wanna be with you

Dion believe me
Nothing is ever easy
And into this life that you're leading
You're lucky you're warm
            when it's freezing

Dion baby oh, oh, oh, Dion baby
One of these nights
I'm gonna feel your breath
Fingers x'd on my chest

Dion you're changing
With every moment pretending
Think of the time we'll be
            spending
It could be never ending

Dion baby oh, oh, oh, Dion baby
Well I wanna be with you
I'd love to be with you
I wanna be with you

Dion baby oh, oh, oh, Dion babyl
Dion baby oh, oh, oh, Dion babyl
Dion baby oh, oh, oh, Dion babyl

© Dionnio Music, administered by Bug reprinted by permission

when I was on tour. On a few occasions, I was able to bring her out to L.A. for a few weeks, or visit her in Tulsa. Trips like these can be expensive, but who can put a price on having your kid next to you on Christmas morning?

Unfortunately, for long distance dads, the size of their pocket books can have a direct effect on the relationship they can sustain with their kids.

In 1986, I was excited about the release of my latest album, "Wild Dogs." My previous album, "Jungle," had been successful and yielded the hit single, "Girls." I think this was the first time Dion saw me on MTV and knew what her dad did for a living. Things were looking up. Once again, I moved to another record label, and I even changed the name of my publishing company to Dionnio Music.

"Wild Dogs," by Dwight

However, just a few weeks before the release of the new album, the head of my record company became the focus of an industry-wide payola scandal. The record label and, with it, "Wild Dogs," seemed to vanish in a puff of smoke. There would be no radio, MTV—or sales. If the problems I had before were a bad dream, this was a nightmare! I was "back in the torture boat," watching my career sink. Simultaneously, another unforeseen ordeal was surfacing.

Linda had remarried, and suddenly my daughter was calling another person "dad." So, what did that make me, "dad number one" or "dad number two"? I'm sure that there are a lot of step-dads who do a great job and are sensitive to the predicament of the child's biological father, but I still had trouble hearing my daughter calling someone else "dad." It was a very unsettling feeling. Talking to Dion on the phone became increasingly awkward. She seemed inhibited, as if someone might overhear her say the wrong thing. It made me feel even more distant.

I was really fortunate, in that I actually had no problems with Dion's step-father. Still, even though his presence in the household turned out to be relatively short, it was just hard to step aside and allow someone else to teach, discipline and assume the position of a fatherly role model to my child. But, after all, I really had no choice in the matter. This awkward predicament is an enormous weight carried almost exclusively on the shoulders of estranged fathers, although I am sure that separated mothers and grandparents experience their own unique anguish. For those who haven't experienced it, the emotions involved are impossible to describe.

Ironically, the "communication card house" continued to tilt. Since she was a baby, Dion had been close to my girlfriend, Susan. Susan is a great person and a real talent. She sang on a number of my records and was well-known as a member of the group The Cowsills. Dion and Susan would talk about "girl things" that I might otherwise never have been aware of. But when, after nearly nine years, Susan and I separated,

Dion's Birthday Poem

You were far too old

when you were seven

now I find that you're eleven.

It's hard to see my baby snake

grow up so fast when I'm away.

Our kittens try to make us famous

and if we fail, their hearts

won't blame us.

But even when you're eighty-two

your dad will still, love, love, love, you.

yet another source of communication with Dion collapsed.

Phone calls were becoming less than rewarding as well. Trying to carry on an intimate and personal conversation with a rock video blaring in the background was a task in itself. At this point, with visits not practical either, I still wanted to, somehow, maintain my presence in Dion's life. I entered a short phase of sending Dion elaborate letters. I spent a lot of time trying to make them amusing and clever. I included numerous intricate drawings, poems and occasional surprises.

Working on the letters really felt good up until it was time to mail them. But the minute I dropped them in post box, it was like they disappeared. They were gone. The same was true at Christmas and on her birthdays. As soon as the last gift was packed and ready to be mailed, I'd start feeling depressed. That Christmas or birthday was over—for me. I rarely got to see her face when she opened her presents.

I was always thrilled to receive any letter from Dion. However, in this "Nintendo-MTV world" we live in, most pre-teens don't invest huge amounts of time writing letters. While I treasured every one, my daughter's letters proved to be of little value as far as figuring out what was really happening in her life. In one letter, I might learn two things: Yes, she got my last post card and "Everything A Dad Ever Wanted To Know—About Her Newest Video Game!"

I kept thinking there must be a better way to approach this communication thing. And what could I do that would elevate my visibility in Dion's mind when I'm half a continent away? I decided to try an experiment.

I decided to put myself in my daughter's place. I thought back to when I was about her age. I remembered how a teacher surprised my class with a test on

"Bitty Bacawn,"
by Dwight

the first day of school. I recalled the sighs and groans that filled the classroom. But as the tests were being passed out, I began to hear giggling—and then laughter—because this test was *different*. It was fun. It asked personal questions, like, "Who would you like for your boyfriend or girlfriend?" It was the only time I remember everyone in my class *enjoying* a test. I knew my daughter liked to read, write and draw. So, why not? I decided to create my own test, just for her. The idea was so simple, it seemed too good to be true.

I thought it would be a fun and personal questionnaire from dad, but it really turned out to be much, much more.

Without thinking much about it, I pulled out a sheet of notebook paper and just started writing questions. I kept them simple. (Yes or no, fill in the blanks, etc.) Most of all, I tried to come up with questions about things we had in common in our personal relationship. I also included questions that I hoped she would think were funny or might spark her imagination.

I thought if I made it light and entertaining, now and then I could toss in a question about something I really wanted an answer to. I called it "The Dad's Questions For Dion Test." Before sealing the envelope, I had another thought. I took a second envelope, put a stamp and my address on it and slipped it in along with the test. The idea was to make it easier for Dion to get it back to me. Then, just before mailing the test, I had a startling revelation. I didn't have that depressing "letter disappears into nowhere" feeling. This time, it was dif-

Dear Dad, pg 1
I can't wait till summer it will be fun.
Disneyezed DADS Dionne

Dionne's Letter

ferent. In fact, it was exciting! As I placed the test in the mail, I felt like the kid sending away for the "secret decoder ring" from the back of the cereal box!

With the holidays around the corner, I had already begun my neurotic quest to purchase every crazy toy on the planet. After all, it had been my duty to supply Dion with an endless army of Cabbage Patch Kids, dolls that did things that scared me, and a host of mind-altering Japanese gizmos.

Rusty nails in my eyes would be better than my Dion being let down at Christmas. And, God forbid, I might screw up that one annual golden opportunity when fathers are, for a minute, most likely to garner their child's attention and reaffirm the concept that dad *really exists*. I thought, if this "Dad's Test" idea worked, I might try another, and maybe find out what she really wanted for Christmas. I didn't have to wait very long.

In a matter of days—bang! There it was, at my door. The test—sent back and completed! I couldn't believe it. It was great! In fact, it was supercalifragilisticexpialidocious! Apparently, the test had struck a nerve with young Ms. Twilley. She seemed to instantly understand the whole concept. At this point, I knew I was on to something!

I got such a kick out of reading Dion's forthright answers! I learned much more from this single questionnaire than I had from all of her previous letters. Immediately, I envisioned how I could easily expand and improve upon the next test. A host of new questions filled my mind—things I might never have gotten around to asking her in a letter or on the phone.

At first, I was patting myself on the back over the success of the test. My "dadly" head had swollen to such proportions that it was no longer easy passing through doorways! Finally, though, I had to force myself to come down to Earth long enough to realize that my daughter was as much a part of this as I was. Wow! We were doing this *together!* Still, I took great satisfaction in knowing that *this* Christmas I *would* know exactly which Japanese gizmos to grab—and maybe even what they were!

I was soon to discover that there is something very special and magical about the world of the Dad's Tests. It's a world where it's safe to say anything you want. It's a world where make-believe is

"Me, Daddy, My Dog," by Dionne

okay. It's a world where dreams and fantasies are born. It's a world where parent and child meet on equal ground. It's a world where there's always enough time, and distance doesn't matter. It's a world without barriers. It's a perfect world.

Unlike the letters I had sent in the past, the Dad's Tests never disappear, and believe me, they're much more than most keepsakes. They're a chronicle of a very special relationship I now have with my daughter.

Coincidentally, just days after her first completed test arrived, I received a rare phone call from Dion. I'll never forget the excitement in her voice: "Dad! Send more tests!"

LOOKING AT
THESE TESTS

Right off the bat, I want to make one thing clear. I never thought of myself as any kind of child psychologist or expert with kids. In fact, if you totalled up all the days I've been able to spend with my daughter since she was born, I'm sure it would unfortunately fall short of a year's time. So whatever I can do to add even an hour or two to that precious year is well worth it to me. I look at these tests as "quality absentee time." The bottom line is, these questionnaires have been fun for me and fun for my daughter. When there are more than a thousand miles between you and your child—or another obstacle that may feel like the equivalent—fun is a rare and cherished commodity. This is what I hope to pass on to you.

I realize that the thought of a rock songwriter whose first hit song's lyrics were "You ain't, you ain't, you ain't got no lover" trying to write a book about parenting is, at the very least, humorous. Regardless, I will try to shed some light on this goofy idea that turned out to be a landmark event in my world as a distant dad.

Before I started writing this book, I thought it would be a good idea to go back and review all the

> " I look at these tests as quality absentee time. "

Dionne's "An alien from Mars," from 1991.

tests I had sent to Dion. Besides, it had always been fun to pull out an old test and "relive the moment."

So I go to my closet and yank down the large cardboard box where I keep all of Dion's photos, letters and various memorabilia. Sorting through stacks of drawings and Christmas cards, I uncover a few, forgotten tests from years past. My search is periodically distracted by drawings of indescribable creatures that were supposed to be me. Finally, I believe I've located all of the "Dad's Tests."

Now here I sit, looking at these tests. As I lay them out in front of me and begin to thumb through them, a number of things are going through my mind. The worst thing is, I wish I had come up with the idea years earlier, when she first began to read and write. Fortunately, these tests have at least provided me with a unique and invaluable chronicle of my relationship with my daughter over the last few years, and the promise of much more in the years ahead. I know that when I finally pack my bags for the old folks home, the Dad's Tests will not be left behind.

Also, I'm surprised to find nearly seventy-five pages of tests, beginning with the first, which was merely the front and back of a single sheet of notebook paper. I recall how I quickly learned that the staunch demand for longer and more challenging tests had to be met. This called for much experimentation and imagination.

In subsequent tests, I began to add *Where's Waldo?* type drawings and ambitious dot-to-dot adventures. I kept adding spices and other ingredients to the "test recipe." The forces of supply and demand eventually dictated that one hundred questions would be the acceptable length for what constituted a *real* Dad's Test. Under a hundred questions, dad was holding out; over a hundred seemed a bit much. Hence, "The Dad's Questions For Dion Test" evolved into "100 Questions From Dad." I considered the evolution from a single sheet of notebook paper to as many as eighteen pages, complete with color-photocopy cover in a clear plastic binder, to be a milestone in "long-distance-dadness."

Dionne as Cleopatra, Halloween, 1990

I think of the four or five hours spent over a couple of weeks preparing each test as a high-yield investment. However, I recall many times I'd stall out around question number seventy-five. How could I come up with twenty-five more questions that would keep her attention and have any real meaning? Somehow, though, after the required amount of "pacing and erasing," I found I could always nudge my way to the century mark, and, when I'd finish, I'd think to myself, "What was I worried about? Dad conquers another test!"

And of course, once a test was in the mail, a number of questions I wished I would have asked would instantly come to mind!

When I stand back and look at all the tests as a whole, I ask myself, "What was I trying to do?" First, I guess I was just trying to communicate with my daughter all the silly little things; subjects too trivial to con-

Dad on stage,
by Dionne

stitute a letter or a phone call. If there were things that we could share the same sense of humor about, that was, at least, a beginning.

The game-like environment of these recurring quizzes created a kind of "synthesized camaraderie" that would more likely be present between a parent and child in the atmosphere of day-to-day chatter under the same roof. That's one of the reasons why I like to ask her about her pets and things that surround her, and have always included recurring references to subjects that are private jokes no one else would understand. "Baby Snakes" and "The Little Man In Chinatown" have been staple themes.

My second intention was, of course, to find out what was happening in Dion's life. Occasionally, I was looking for a serious answer to a serious question, but the little things, like her favorite cookie, were just as important.

At a glance, here's a random list of things I've learned from the Dad's Tests over the years:

1: On Halloween of 1990, my daughter was Cleopatra.

2: How to find warps in Mario III.

3: My daughter knows that drugs are dangerous and stupid.

4: Receiving any kind of clothes for Christmas is an abomination.

5: Science is my daughter's favorite subject in school.

6: Liver should be buried in the backyard—not served for dinner!

7: She is very happy where she lives.

8: Her cat "Princess" plays a great piano!

9: If anyone ever hurt my daughter, she wouldn't hesitate to tell me about it.

10: My daughter has a great sense of humor. She is sweet, intelligent and will always be my "baby snake."

Now, here is a list of things I think Dion may have learned from the tests:

1: Her dad is willing to spend the time required to construct these tests for her.

2: Dad's cat "Mow" likes to type letters and send them to her cat, "Princess."

3: How to draw "old Grandpa Snake."

4: Dad speaks "Nintendo."

5: Dad can be pretty silly.

6: How she and her dad can communicate through their art.

7: Dad is concerned for her happiness.

8: Dad is interested in the way she looks at things.

9: Dad wants to be a part of her life despite the distance between us.

10: Her dad love, love, love, love, love, loves her.

One could argue that I could have learned about Cleopatra on Halloween through a letter or phone call. But I'm sure I never would have known how well Princess plays piano!

I know I'll have to face the fact that, sometime in the future, these questionnaires could lose

GRANDPA SNAKE

"State Fair,"
by Dwight

their appeal. It's hard to predict how the Dad's Tests will weather the teenage years.

Dads have a lot to compete with out there. Just being a teen automatically crowds a kid's social calendar. With shopping malls, homework, school activities, sports and, inevitably, boyfriends and girlfriends, a dad—especially a long distance dad—can end up with a pretty small piece of the pie! All in all, this can be a pretty hard pill to swallow. But, the fact is, it wasn't your child's idea to place his or her father away from home in the first place. With so many new doors waiting to be opened, forfeiting special holidays and the magic and romance of summer to spend time with the "old man" may become less and less palatable. Walking that "teenage tightrope," teetering between the security of "just being a kid" and the lure of adulthood is an adventure in itself. All this will, no doubt, be tugging away from the boring chore of writing to pop. ("What do I say to this ancient dude?")

By customizing and adjusting my tests for a more preoccupied recipient, I'm hoping they'll survive through a time when they may be more valuable than ever. Perhaps the new fast and "user-friendly" routine of these novel questionnaires may earn that ever-so-important moment of attention and verify that dad is not only alive, but eats at Burger King with Elvis! Who knows? The old Dad's Test might be a welcome relief in the midst of college exams.

Lastly, what about that awkward moment when a friend or family member inquires about your separated child? Instead of the sad scenario they might expect, dazzle them with a glance at your latest test! These are not treasures to be buried. Dion and I have no qualms about letting the world know what the Snake family looks like on Christmas day. Besides the fact that we're both really a couple of hams, I really get a kick out of showing people the quizzes. The idea of pulling out old letters or photos pales next to the epic blockbuster impact of a Dad's Test!

I'm pretty sure that my method could work for a lot of people, and, while the impact of Dad's Test idea may not change the world as we know it, I'm quite sure that thousands of cats and dogs will both improve their piano playing skills and feel less inhibited about writing letters to their feline and canine friends across the country!

GETTING YOUR FEET WET

Now that you are ready to "take the plunge," I will try to guide you through the construction of your first "Dad's Test."

It's important to remember that these tests are an ongoing experiment. You may find a different approach that I haven't even thought of. Of course, the content of your quiz will vary according to your child's age and sex, but I think children's appreciation for the attention the tests provide is universal. As soon as your child is able to read and write, he or she is a candidate for the Dad's Test. Before you begin, you may want to take a look at any letters, schoolwork or other examples of your son's or daughter's writing skills. This will help you choose words that your youngster will understand.

You may want to begin by thinking of a name for your first test. I encourage you to select a title that both relates the idea of the quiz and makes it clear that it is personalized—just between you and your child. For example, "The Dad's Test For Susan" or "25 Questions For Michael From Dad." If you feel the word "test" may be intimidating, remember, there are no rules! The "tests" have worked well for me, but you may want to

> **"**
> Keep your first test short, 20 to 40 questions.
> **"**

"Complete the
drawing," from
Dad's Test, 1993.

call your quiz "Karen's Fun Book From Dad" or "Dad's Question Game For Craig."

I suggest that you keep your first questionnaire reasonably short—say twenty to forty inquiries. Make a rough list of any questions that you're sure you want to ask. List the names of your child's pets, friends, toys, games and any other subjects he or she can easily relate to. Use the lists to help create your questions. Once you have selected a title, you are ready for the major hurdle—the first question.

Start with very light inquiries which immediately—and clearly—demonstrate that the test is supposed to be *fun*.

1. *"What is your favorite T.V. show?"*
2. *"What is your dog's favorite T.V. show?"*

If you have any questions of a serious nature, make sure they are well-insulated by lots of silliness! Within a chain of wacky inquiries, a spontaneous answer to a serious question is more likely. (On the other hand, don't be surprised if a goofy question receives an unexpected serious response.)

As your quiz takes form, it's important that you keep it interesting. This is crucial in keeping your child's attention and can be accomplished by constantly changing question styles and adding artistic activities.

Examples of different question styles

TRUE/FALSE

You should never eat anything bigger than your own head.
True_____ False_____

MULTIPLE CHOICE

What does your room look like?
A. Neat and clean_____
B. Not too bad_____
C. Disaster area_____

YES/NO

Do you help your mom around the house?
Yes_____ No_____

YES/NO/OTHER OPTIONS

Do you like school?
Yes_____ No_____ A little _____ A lot_____

WHICH IS BEST

Which is best?
Hamburger_____ Hot Dog_____

FILL IN THE BLANK

There was a little man in _____ town.

NAME THINGS

What would be a good name for a home video for
us to make?_____

SYMBOL IN THE BOX

Put a "♥" in the box if you love it.
Put a "☺" in the box if you like it.
Put a "☹" in the box if you don't like it.
Put a "X" in the box if you hate it.
Liver [ ] Apple Juice [ ] Popcorn [ ]

LIST

List the names of all of your pets.
1._____
2._____
3._____

"Duck," by Dionne

FILL-IN-THE-BLANK-STORY

    There once was a _____ girl who lived in the _____ town of _____.

CHALLENGE

    Write your name the best you can

_____

    Write your name the worst you can.

_____

Adding art activities will also help add interest to your questionnaire. While you may or may not have any artistic skills yourself, it's not too hard to use a straight edge to draw a box, trace a square object or to simply write "Draw A Picture Of Your Dog." Kids love to draw, and there seems to be no limit to their imagination. To fulfill this appetite over the past three years, I have made some bizarre and wide ranging requests.

"Draw the Snake Family At Christmas"
"Draw the Worst Insect"
"Draw a Singing Fish Head"
"Draw an Alien From Mars"
"Draw the Flea Christmas Parade"
"Draw Rudolph the Red-Nosed Mallard"

Never in the entire realm of "dad-testology" has a single one of these challenges failed to be met and conquered, often with mind-boggling results. I find it interesting and rewarding that, even from a distance, I'm able to fuel my daughter's imagination, and then have my own outlook broadened. Now when I close my eyes and envision an alien from Mars, only Dion's unearthly illustration comes to mind.

Additional (more Earthbound) artistic requests might be:

> **"**
> The test
> is supposed
> to be fun.
> **"**

HOUSE	MOTHER	ROOM
SCHOOL	SIBLINGS	MONSTERS
FRIENDS	RELATIVES	ANIMALS
PETS	XMAS TREE	SANTA
TOYS	FAMILY CAR	CARTOON CHARACTERS

Throughout this book, I have used samples of art that Dion and I have used to correspond with each other over the years. Dion's rendering of "Princess and Her Servants" certainly rivals my "Cat With Sunglasses." I see a more than coincidental similarity in their styles. Don't be intimidated by all of the art in my tests. Your cartoonish doodle or mindless scribbling could easily invoke a greater response from your youngster than a carefully planned out drawing. Remember:. . . . "Stick People" are funny!

"Squiggles" can also be fun. It's easy for anyone to draw a couple of squiggly lines and request: "Complete the Squiggle." The results are impossible to predict. Also, try drawing heads with no faces, houses with no doors or windows and request: "Complete the Drawing."

Participating in your child's art can create an unusual camaraderie. The same is true with other forms of participation-style questions, like the "fill-in-the-blank stories." However, it is a little embarrassing when the kid's work turns out better than yours!

Try experiments. On one of my latest tests, I tried making a crossword puzzle using words and

"Cat with Sunglasses," by Dwight

Stick people
are funny!
"Zorro,"
by Dwight

names that were common Dad's Test lingo. Completing the puzzle, I had learned two things:

1. I will never try to create another crossword puzzle as long as I live.

2. It *was* different, and she'll probably get a kick out of it. You may be a whiz at making puzzles. I'll stick to heads with no faces.

Of course, Dion loved the crossword puzzle, and requested more!

I'm well aware that many dads have more than one estranged child, and having more than one child may create a few obstacles and call for additional effort. Naturally, you will want to make sure that your attention is equally distributed between your children. While I can't speak from experience, I can at least suggest a few hints that might lighten the load.

• Make a photocopy of your test and send the same test to all your children at once, with personalized title pages.

• Same process as above, only completely omit a few questions, leaving the spaces blank. After copying, just add in those few questions with personalized inquiries according to age, gender, etc.

• Send a test to your eldest child. Early in the test, request: "Tell your little sister that the next test dad sends will be for her." Later in the test, ask: "Did your remeber to tell your sister that dad is sending her a test next?" Later in the test, ask: "Since you are getting to be such a grown up boy, can you help your little sister with her dad's test when it comes?"

• Split one test in half. "Fifty Questions for Rocky and Chanti." The first 25 for your eldest, followed by a request that the test then be passed to the younger child, perhaps ending with questions the two can do together.

• Send a "smorgasbord-test." One test to be passed from child to child. Each question has multiple, personalized spaces for each child's answer.
Here's an example:

What is your favorite video game?
Phil's aswer_____
Ed's answer_____
Wendy's answer_____

Hopefully, all the preceding suggestions and advice will be of some value in helping you with your first Dad's Test! Here are some additional tips to make your

"The All New Dad's Questions for Dion Test"

A WITCH   A GHOST   BUD

TOBY   PEE-PEE   MARIO

early questionnaires more effective and ensure their return.

When your first quiz is completed and ready to be mailed, don't forget to include instructions. Avoid a lengthy letter that might dilute your intent here. Instead, write a simple note:

Dear Carrie,
Here is the "Dad's Test For Carrie 1994." Please answer the questions as best you can.
When you are finished, put the test in the red envelope and mail it back to me.
I hope you have fun with this test!
Love,
Dad

You probably will want to continue to include these instructions in succeeding tests until you're sure the routine has been established. If possible, a few phone calls before and after your child receives the first test will help further explain the test and, hopefully, get your child excited about the idea.

Another way that may help expedite the initial test process is using a brightly colored envelope for the return of the test. I strongly feel that the whole "Dad's Test" concept would be crippled without the all-important, self-addressed-postage-paid return envelope. The bright red envelope will be easily identifiable from your instructions. I've found it to be a simple and invaluable aid to my daughter for returning her completed test to me. 100 questions lost in the "black hole" of "toy box hell" are no good to anyone!

Depending on the age of your son or daughter, a small amount of participation from the custodial parent may be required in the early stages of "dad-testing." You may have accidentally used a word that your child doesn't understand or can't read. And, even with your

"
Subjects are as numerous as the problems and achievements of childhood.
"

prepared, colored return envelope, it might require a more responsible hand to drop it in the mail box. In most cases, I would hope the custodial parent would welcome positive communication between his or her son or daughter and the separated parent, simply because it's healthy for the child to have contact with both parents.

In my case, Dion was already ten when I began sending the tests, and, fortunately, automatically locked into the process. Linda told me that, when a test would arrive, Dion would mysteriously disappear into her room. The next day the test would be mailed with nothing said to mom. On other occasions, Dion would show her the latest rendering of "The Snake Family at Christmas," or, out of the blue, make strange inquiries like "How do you spell dad's middle name?"

A sample cover.

Initially, establishing the routine of your tests may be a little awkward for all the parties involved. Just remember to keep any explanations simple and positive. Hopefully, it will not be long before your questionnaires will be as they were intended—just between you and your child.

After subsequent tests have established the routine, you may want to embellish or expand the title to sustain interest and to focus on particular subjects. A cover page can be a nice touch. It can capture "the pupil's" attention and make your test look more "official." Write the title of your test in BIG letters on the top of a clean sheet of paper (possibly colored paper), then affix a photo or two underneath (shots of you, your child or pets are trustworthy subjects). Try a drawing. You'll be asking your kid to draw; show your son or daughter you're willing to meet them on equal ground. Zip over to the corner copy store and make a couple of color prints. Be creative. Your "Norman Rockwell Meets Salvadore Dali" cover page will give your test personality and will also be a great memento for you and your sprout.

The cover page design may be motivated by your more elaborate test title or title that addresses a specific subject. Here are some examples:

- **"The All New Dad's Test for Jan"**

- **"50 Questions from Dad—The Special Edition"**

- **"The 1994 Christmas Test for Tommy"**
  This test will serve to arm you with the strategic insight to face the ever changing arsenal of G.I. Joe, video and sports paraphernalia, and, thus, help you survive the annual siege at Toys 'R Us.

- **"The Johnnie's Trip to Texas Test"**
  Your child may be coming to visit you or taking some other trip (i.e. summer camp for the first time) which could be the source of some anxiety. This test may help smooth either road.

- **"Linda's 10th Birthday Test from Dad"**
  What is the perfect gift? How does she feel about growing older? This test is another way of asserting your presence on her birthday from a distance.

- **"Dad's Test to Joe About Scooter"**
  This test could address the loss of a friend, relative or beloved pet.

As you can see, the possibilities for tests that focus on specific subjects are as numerous as the problems and achievements of childhood.

After you get through your first couple of tests, you'll start to get a feel for what works, what doesn't work and what *really* works. When something really works, don't hesitate to repeat the same type of question or activity again and again in future tests.

Sometimes, you may be surprised by a question that receives little or no response. Remember, a youngster's entire view of life can change on an hourly basis. Wait a while, and try the same question again on a later quiz. The results may surprise you.

Remember to seek out topics that are exclusive between you and your child, as they help to create a string of reminders that you are a real father—and a *real person*.

Dionne's "Pals"

It's understandable that your tests will grow in length. In this multi-media world, a couple of pieces of paper with questions on them may not continue to earn the same interest as what your test will likely evolve into, perhaps something like the shiny, thick booklet with the color-laserprint cover that I now use. Who knows? In a couple of years, I may have to go "hardback!"

However, it's ironic how, as your child gets older, it's possible that the tests may start to get shorter, and eventually return to their original twenty to forty question length to accommodate for the shrinking time allotted us distant dads. Once again, we're back to trying to keep their attention.

Perhaps, soon, computers and other interactive devices will come to the rescue, with "digital dads" zapping their tests across the country, spitting out wild, high-tech graphics and offering new mental challenges.

I've found that it's kind of a funny Catch-22. On the one hand, as your tests get longer, you can get tired or bored coming up with more and more questions. But, on the other hand, once you've received back the completed test, poring over the answers can be such a gas, that you end up wishing you had scrawled pages and pages more.

Somewhere along the line, I'm sure you will find yourself, as I have, nearing the hundred question mark (or whatever personal goal you've set for your test), and then experiencing that special moment when you feel you are no longer capable of rational thought, let alone coming up with any more questions. Usually, the best resolve is to simply put it away until tomorrow. Give it a rest! Then, when you're relaxed and ready to carry on, a glance through the random list of question categories that follows might inspire an idea. For further assistance in constructing your test, consult the following chapter, *"Checklist and Troubleshooting Guide."*

"Freddy the Frog and a Friend," by Dionne

"Menagerie," by Dwight

100 CATEGORIES FOR DAD'S QUESTIONS

1. School situations
2. Friends and aquaintances
3. Social situations
4. Sex and sexuality
5. Peer pressures
6. Adolescence and puberty
7. Death or serious illness
8. Pets/death of a pet
9. Hobbies and collections
10. Living conditions
11. Sleeping habits
12. Dreams and nightmares
13. Food likes and dislikes
14. Cooking
15. Sweets and snacks
16. Pizza
17. Dinosaurs
18. Anything Disney
19. Entertainment
20. Movies
21. Movie stars
22. T.V. shows
23. T.V. stars
24. Music
25. Music stars
26. Games
27. Cartoons
28. Comics
29 Books
30. Toys
31. Theme parks
32. Sports
33. Sports teams and stars
34. MTV
35. UFO's
36. Ghosts
37. Drugs and alcohol
38. Smoking
39. Parental separation stress
40. Responsibility
41. Religion
42. Holidays
43. Family awareness
44. Morality
45. Aesthetics

46. Cleanliness
47. Doctors, dentists and shots
48. Glasses and braces
49. Bed wetting
50. Birth and babies
51. Siblings
52. Safety
53. Discipline
54. Laws and rules
55. Patriotism
56. Gossip and rumors
57. Manners
58. Fighting and roughhousing
59. Pillow fights
60. Food fights
61. Mud wrestling
62. Money
63. Fears and insecurities
64. Depression
65. Boredom
66. Hostilities
67. Abuse or harassment
68. Good and evil
69. Heroes and villains
70. Wealth and status
71. Racism and prejudice
72. Malls and shopping
73. Fads and fashion

74. Phones and phone numbers
75. Chores
76. Summer camp
77. Nature
78. The environment
79. Places visited
80. Places to visit
81. Space travel
82. Cars, planes and trains
83. Gift desires
84. Possible careers
85. Current events/news
86. War and famine
87. Computers
88. The weather
89. Slang
90. Santa and his elves
91. Exercise
92. Jokes
93. Complaints
94. Art
95. Clubs
96. Jumping on beds
97. Frogs
98. Warts and pimples
99. Spills and messes
100. . . . and
       DAD'S TESTS!

CHECKLIST AND TROUBLESHOOTING GUIDE

While constructing your test, take advantage of this handy checklist and guide. This list could help solve a problem, provide motivation or at least establish a direction that may afford you the same success I have enjoyed with my questionnaires.

> **"**
> Make sure
> you keep
> your tests
> interesting.
> **"**

1. I DON'T HAVE TIME FOR THIS!

Sure you do! Use a yellow legal pad. Place it in plain sight on a bedside table or some place where you like to relax. Get into a habit of adding just a few questions to your test each day. It will only take a couple of minutes of your time daily, perhaps before bed or during your lunch break. Your questions will be more well thought out if you don't feel pressured, and you'll be surprised how quickly your quiz is completed. Remember, your test can be as long—or as short—as you like.

2. WILL I ALWAYS BE WORKING ON THESE TESTS?

Hardly! Two or three good tests per year should keep you in touch with your child and supply you with plenty of information—perhaps before Christmas, dur-

ing the summer or in the fall. If you want to do more, great!

3. MY KID HATES TESTS!

So, don't call it one! Give your quiz a happy or exciting title. "Secret Questions For Sarah" or "Dad's Amazing Crazy Quiz Game."

4. USE A PENCIL!

You'll save a lot of time correcting an error or changing a question when it can be easily erased.

5. MAKE IT EASY TO READ

Try to print your questions using easy-to-read CAPITAL letters. Of course, avoid using words above your child's vocabulary or reading skill. Shy away from typing, if possible. It's too much like a "real" test. However, a typed test is better than no test. If you and your child are into computers, you can use a PC to construct your test. You might even

"Plane Sense,"
by Dwight
•••••••••➤

want to go "direct-to-disk" and send a "floppy-test" to your digital son or daughter! But remember, if you use a typewriter or computer, more creativity or silliness may be required to keep your test from taking on too much of an "academic" appearance. Don't forget, your test should be intimate—and *fun*!

6. MAKE IT FUN!

Why? So, to quote my daughter, "It's not boring, like a letter!" This is especially important if there are some serious questions you would like to get honest and uninhibited answers to. Insulate your sober inquiries with lots of lighthearted and silly exchanges. A forthright answer to a "heavy" question is more likely to surface when surrounded by queries like "DO YOU THINK CHRISTMAS TREES SHOULD BE DECORATED WITH PIZZA?"

Complete the squiggle, from "The All New Bigger and Better Than Ever 1991 Dad's Questions for Dionne Test: The Next Generation."

7. WHAT IS FUN?

Things from your child's world—questions about your son or daughter's friends, pets, toys, etc. "CAN YOU FIND THE FIRST WARP IN SUPER MARIO?" "DRAW A PICTURE OF YOUR DOG READING A BOOK."

8. IMAGINATION

Make sure you have included some questions or tasks that will allow your child to use his or her imagination. "DRAW A PICTURE OF AN ALIEN FROM MARS." "HOW OLD DO YOU THINK SANTA CLAUSE IS?"

"Mom's Rules,"
by Dionne

9. HAVE CRAYON WILL TRAVEL

Don't forget the art! A Dad's Test without requests for drawings is like peanut butter without jelly! If thousands of dads ask for pictures of "The Alien From Mars," maybe we'll find out what the little bugger really looks like!

10. DOES DAD REALLY EXIST?

Or is he just "the guy who sends stuff on holidays or birthdays?" Try to think of things you have in common, such as places or experiences you have shared or things that only you and your child will remember. "WHAT WAS THE MOST FUN THING WE DID AT AT DISNEYLAND?" These questions will remind your child that "dad" really does exist! He took you to Disneyland, remember?

11. THE REPETITION GAME

Choose a common experience, like a song you may have sung together or a story you shared. Each time you send a new test, find a different way of asking about the same experience. This can become your own "private joke" with your child. "A SPOONFUL OF SUGAR HELPS THE_____GO DOWN." "TRUE OR FALSE: A SPOONFUL OF SALT HELPS THE MEDICINE GO DOWN."

12. WE'RE TALKIN' SHORT ATTENTION SPAN . . .

Make sure you keep your test interesting. This can be accomplished by mixing a wide variety of question styles. Use a "multiple choice" question followed by a "true or false" and then a "draw a picture in the box" request. Try to create surprises. "DID YOU THINK THE LAST QUESTION WAS STUPID?" "WRITE YOUR NAME BACKWARDS."

13. MESSAGES

Messages can be subtly placed into your questions. Perhaps there's something you'd like your youngster to know—perhaps something as simple as the fact that you miss them. "DO YOU THINK IF I DIDN'T LIVE SO FAR AWAY I WOULDN'T MISS YOU SO MUCH?"

14. DAMAGE CONTROL

I would strongly suggest you avoid questions that might draw other parties into what should be a very private dialogue between you and your child. "DO YOU HELP MOM AROUND THE HOUSE?" is okay, but "IS YOUR STEP-FATHER EVER MEAN TO YOU?" might create problems. "IS ANYONE EVER MEAN TO YOU?" is much better. In general, stay away from names. Your harmless intentions could invite interference from an unexpected source. There's always the possibility you'll receive an answer

"Nativity Scene," by Dionne

you're really not happy with—or even one that alarms you. But, at least, then you'll know, and can take appropriate action.

15. GETTING YOUR TEST BACK

By enclosing the *all important* postage-paid-self-addressed return envelope, you instantly limit the potential of third-party participation, which can often be negatively apathetic—or just plain negative. The pre-prepared envelope allows your child the privacy and independence to simply answer the questions and place them in the mail without any additional adult supervision. Leaving the responsibility of postage and finding envelopes to your child—or a third party—can seriously jeopardize the completion and return of the test!

"The Professor" by Dwight

16. USE YOUR OLD TESTS

After you've made your way through a few questionnaires, take advantage of your old tests! Review the quizzes for questions to be followed up on, repeat activities that were well received and create new questions based on some of the unexpected responses. This will give your tests continuity and keep the dialogue meaningful!

17. DON'T BE A TEACHER!

When you receive a completed test back from your child, avoid the temptation to correct grammar or spelling errors! This is not what these tests are about. Such scrutiny will take away the fun and inhibit future candid and frank responses. If anything, "grade" your child's candor and imagination. Circle particularly honest or open answers and send back a copy of the test with big red "A+!"

18. EXPERIMENT

Anything goes—maybe better than you think!

"Elf and Dog," by Dwight

SPINOFFS AND SPECIAL GUESTS

Much like a successful television series, the Dad's Tests have created "spinoffs," like when Danny Thomas was pulled over for speeding by a then-unknown Sheriff Andy Taylor of Mayberry or when Richie Cunningham and The Fonz traded laughs with Laverne and Shirley. It's interesting how a question or subject included in a test may take on a life of its own. The nature of these spinoffs seems to be that they just appear unexpectedly. The very first spinoff that I experienced was, perhaps, the best example.

I think it was about the time I was waiting for the return of the second or third test I had sent to Dion. I was having a lot of fun thinking of the questions and waiting to see what kind of response they would yield. It was all still pretty new to me, and what I might have thought was a great question could receive a "dud" response, while an answer to a blatant, straight-forward question would have me rolling on the floor.

I remember picking up the mail and finding a parcel from Dion. Right away I felt that adrenalin rush and thought, "Aah, this must be the latest test." But then I noticed that something wasn't right. The package didn't appear to be large enough to contain the test. I opened

> **"** A question in a test may take on a life of its own. **"**

A Few ?'s for DAD.

Whats the name of?   fill in
1. My turtle — Godzilla
2. my hamster — Samster   the Hamster
3. my mini Dog — Bud
4. My Large Dog — Toby
5. My cat — Princess
6. my Ducks — Mohawk   + Beethoven

Hints to Nicknames 4 Tobster
1. Just Tint   5. Prim
2. Sam   6. Bohee
3. Buddirick III   Bee

This is talking about you.
My favorite board game is: Monopoly
My favorite nintendo game is: Monopoly
My fav. food is: Pizza
My fav. Snack is: Coneys
My fav. dessert is: Oreo
My fav. animal is: Cat
My fav. pet is: Mow
My fav. Stars: Wayne & Garth
My fav. Movie: Waynes World $ $ $
My fav. Show: Star Trek the Next Generation
My fav. hobby: Making Tests For My Daughter

Box of CHICKENS

TEST
name each

TREE with
INVISABLE MAN

O-ZAK
FROM THE
PLANET
TWILO

ODDIE BOD RUDY

the Budster

▲ Dionne's "A Few Questions
  for Dad" Test.

it, completely oblivious to the revelation I was about to experience. I couldn't believe my eyes! Never in a thousand years would I have expected what I was now holding in my hands: "A FEW QUESTIONS FOR DAD." Dion had created her own test for me to answer!

After picking my mouth up off the floor, I felt that the test idea had come full circle. It was kind of a natural evolution, but I never saw it coming.

Periodically I would try little experiments, just to see what might strike a nerve or add some new angle to the tests. Once, I sent Dion a letter explaining that my cat Mow had written to me on Christmas Eve. I enclosed "Mow's Letter" with mine, with the intention of getting her response in the test to follow.

I, MOW The KittY, DO pLEdge to KEEp thiS Sacred OATH, anD To the BEST of my KITTY AbiLitiEs wiLL FulfiLL all duTies set Forth in THIS AGREEmenT:

1. I PromiSe to TRy To SIT in Dad'S Lap EVERy Waking HOuR Of the day.

2. ShouLd HE walk arounD, I wiLL folloW HiM to evEry room in thE houSe.

3. if He getS tOO near THe puPPy, i Will stAnd iN AnotHer rooM ANd cry.

4. If hE laYs DowN, I wILL lAy on his sTomAch aNd kNEad mY paWs On HIs cHeSt aNd puRRR.

5. WheN hE GoeS TO SLeep, i Will PaW aT his eyes, noSE And LiPs until hE letS Me unDeR the coveRS, WHerE i wILL SLeeP beTwEen hiS LeGS.

6. if hE gETS uP duRiNG THe NighT, I Will geT UP too, anD theN rePEAt tHe whOLe pRoceSS.

7. I voW to hisS aNd to trY To sWAt the pUppy aT leAst 4 Times A dAy.

8. i PRomiSe TO aTTacK, kiLL, aND eaT All sPiDeRs aNd FLiEs.

9. I will MAke weiRd soUndS WHen i sEE BirDs oUTsiDe tHe WiNdoW.

10. wheN cLeaN launDRy iS plaCed anywHERe in the houSe, iT Is my duTy to coME LaY oN it, befoRE it is folDed.

11. I WiLL, wiThoUt FAil, sPenD at LEast 30 minuTeS a dAY cleANing, swEEping and crEAting aRtisTic desiGNS iN my CAt bOX.

12. I will maKe suRE thaT a nuMBeR of specKS of kiTTy liTTeR aRe uniQuEly pLaCed throughout daD's rOOm on A daiLy baSis.

13. I will faiTHFully conDemN all baLLOONS to deaTh.

14. iT iS MY joB to siT on aNY PAper oR maGaZinE That daD wouLd likE to rEAd or wRiTe on.

15. AnyThing tHat is oPen, thAt I can fiT iNto, I will go iN.

16. WhenEVer daD is usiNg hiS ViDeo caMeRa, I will tRy to bE iN eveRY sCeNe.

17. I pRomiSe neVer to eat mY dRy fOOd unLeSs it is mUShed in wiTH my wet fooD.

18. If aNy stRange doGS or CAts eNtER our yARd, I will waRN dAd by making my taiL 10 tiMes its noRMaL siZE.

19. I will caREfully smeLL eVery nEW iTem tHat is bROught inTo the hoUSe.

20. LastLy, I pROmise thAt whEN I dO somethinG bAd, i will alWayS look reALLy cuTe wHeN I'm doiNg iT.

YouRs truLy,

MOW

Mow's pledge to Dad.

Dear Dion,

On Christmas eve, I couldn't find Mow. It was late at night and I was worried.

Then I thought I heard someone in the office typing. I peeked in, and there was Mow sitting at the computer, typing away.

I thought I was dreaming, but on Christmas morning, I found this letter next to my bed.

DAD

On the next test, I asked Dion the question, "IF YOUR PETS WROTE YOU A LETTER LIKE THE ONE MOW WROTE TO ME, WHAT IS ONE THING THAT TOBY (her dog) MIGHT SAY?" The five questions that followed inquired the same from her other dog, cat, turtle, hamster and ducks.

When the completed test was returned to me, I was a little disappointed. She simply answered, "I'll get him to write one," and then ditto, ditto, ditto to the other five questions. I interpreted this to mean, "Dad, this is a stupid question!"

Once again, about a week later, a thick envelope arrives at my door. To my surprise, I was inundated with pages and pages of crazy comments and promises from all of her pets. Here is a sampling of some of the things that Dion's dogs, cat, turtle, hamster and ducks had to say:

1. "I'll fish for and catch more rocks this year." (Toby)

2. "I'll try to keep track of my beloved rubber ball." (Bud—her puppy)

3. "Practice my hissing lessons once a week with Bud." (Princess—her cat)

4. "I will eat all my food before sunrise." (Samster—the hamster)

5. "I swear to eat all my salad." (Godzilla—her turtle)

6. "To quack all morning until we are fed." (Mohawk & Beethoven—spokesmen for the ducks)

7. ". . . .And most of all, bring in birds, lizards, snakes, mice, and slimy creatures that haven't been discovered yet!" (Princess)

As a result, it is now a commonplace event for our pets to correspond between themselves.

Spinoffs can also be ideas that the tests inspire.

After so many questions asking, "What did you get for Christmas" or "did you like this or that thing that I

```
                    ShMOW TWiLLeY

                     DaD'S RooM

                 LOS AngeLES, CaLIF.


DeaR PrinceSS,

     My namE is SchmOW TwiLLey.  BuT yOu cAN caLL me MOW.  I LiVe
iN LoS AnGeLes, califorNIa wiTh DioN'S daD.

     SoMEtimes I heLP dAd wiTh the teSts he sENds to Dion.  iT'S
my joB to siT on thE paPer when he tRiEs to wRiTe.  ALSo, I muSt
aTTack all peNciLS!

     aNYway, on oNE of the teSTs Dion seNt BacK to dad, I found a
dRAwing of you, so I deciDeD to wRite you a leTTer.

     i aM enClosiNg a phoTo of yourS truLy.  If you caN senD me a
piCtUre of yOU, I will pUt it up neXt to my waTer boWL!

     The woRSt thinG that ever haPPened to mE occuRRed when I was
plaYing.  I was ruNNiNg reaL faST aNd juMPed into tHe baThtub.  I
diDn't kNow the TuB was fuLL of wATER.  It waS like a niGhtMare!
Has aNythiNg liKe this eVer haPPened to yoU?

     I haVE to go noW.  DaD juSt GoT out oF tHe shoWer and I nEEd
to biTe hiS feeT!  NeXT time, i'LL tEll you aBouT thiS crAzy
puPPy nameD "Carrie" thAt liVes in the hOUse.  Write sOOn!



                   YouR FRiend,

                      MOW
```

Mow's Letter

got you for Christmas," a light bulb finally appeared over my head. I decided to videotape the whole Christmas present process.

I showed her the things that I got her and talked about why I thought she might like them. I also let her watch me wrap the gifts and pack them up to be mailed. On a subsequent test, I inquired whether or not she enjoyed my "Christmas Video." Her response was affirmative.

When the following Christmas rolled around—and Dion had her own video camera—my video was now answered by a video of Dion opening her gifts on Christmas morning. After Christmas, the videos were exchanged between us. Like the tests, it at least left us

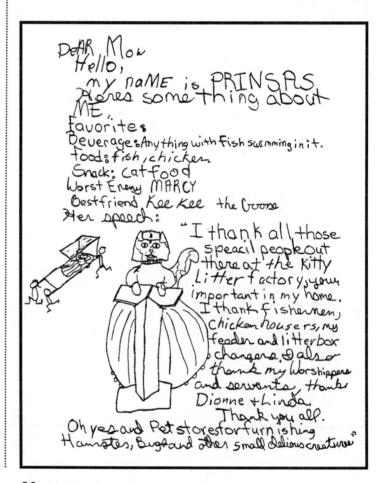

• • • • • • • • • ▶
Princess' Speech

with a memento that captures the Christmas we "sort of" spent together.

It should also be noted that the Dad's Tests also feature visits from "special guest stars."

There are occasional appearances from "Mr. Rat," a plastic rodent who starred in one of our home video movies. Mr. Rat enjoys driving his car and taking his girlfriend Ratina out for pizza.

There is also Julio Mangles, a legendary fictional character who was the subject of another one our father-daughter video productions. The documentary includes various interviews describing Julio as the man responsible for just about every important event in recent history.

When I was a kid, my parents had a funny old forty-five called "The Little Man In Chinatown." It was the flip side of a hit called "The Green Door," recorded in the 50's by Jim Lowe. "Chinatown" repeats the same lyrics over and over, making absolutely no sense.

Dion and I would sing this novelty tune together when she was still just a baby. Since the song was so exclusive to our relationship, I've included some reference to "The Little Man In Chinatown" in virtually every exam.

How to explain "Baby Snakes?" I think it started after a visit to the zoo when Dion was very young. For some unknown reason, Dion suddenly started calling everything

"The Snake Family," by Dionne

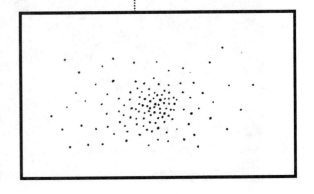

"The Flea Family Portrait," by Dwight

from french fries to pencils "baby snakes." Unexplainable by modern science, this kooky quirk lasted for quite a while. Accordingly, the entire Snake family lives on through the tests.

Oops, I almost forgot to mention "Max-Dog." How could anyone neglect a rock n' roll dog with no legs? Max embarked on his path to fame in 1984 when the song "Max Dog" appeared on my "Jungle" album. During the promotional tour for the album, fans spontaneously began to cut the legs off stuffed animals and neatly sew them up with the intent of tossing them on stage during the concerts. Eventually, a few "Maxes" ended up in Dion's toy box. A character like "Max" is a natural for the tests.

The latest addition, "The Flea Family," has just made their debut. However, no explanation for them is possible, nor needed.

There is no way to predict what may come next. I'm sure that those of you who try my method will experience new and surprising "spinoffs" unique to the rela-

"Where's Mallard?"
by Dwight

tionships the tests can create between you and your child.

I think it's important to let your child know that you are eager to participate in their fantasies just as openly as you would address the hard questions of real life.

Baby snakes are not just imaginary characters. They are real residents of the world that exist exclusively for myself and my daughter in the Dad's Tests.

"Max Dog," by Dwight

PART

THE TESTS

ABOUT THESE TESTS

I sent my first test to Dion when she was a little more than ten years old. The quizzes appear in chronological order, concluding with "100 Questions From Dad 1993," with Dion nearing thirteen. These time capsules represent an on-going exchange. In fact, I'm currently working on a new test, and I'm convinced it will be the best one yet!

Many of you will have the advantage of being able to start using your Dad's Tests when your child is much younger than mine was. Translating a seven year old's "chicken scratch" will most likely be more difficult than the task of "decoding" an answer from an eleven year old. You may want to customize your tests accordingly. Leaving a much bigger space for your seven year old's answer may raise your percentage of comprehension.

While my tests have been cleaned up a little in places to make them more legible, I did want to prepare you for the challenge that may lie in deciphering your child's answers. Answers may be creatively scrawled out over other questions and responses. Words that might be spelled correctly in school are embellished or garbled in a jumbled frenzy. But, by design, all should be fair in the "no-pressure" environment of the test!

With teens, you may want to "streamline" your test to improve its capability of competing with dances, dates and sports.

When prospecting through the hieroglyphic maze of symbols and illustrations, sometimes the true meaning of your child's answer may be overlooked. More than once, I have casually glanced through a test from year's past, and discovered a fact or some subtle humor only Holmes himself would have caught at the time. Perhaps, in the years to come, even more camouflaged messages may appear. Indubitably, a tantalizing mystery!

Of course, the tests are not substitutes for visits, letters or phone calls. Instead, they are a whole new dimension of communication, providing an entirely different level of interaction. Ultimately, this methodology may have a positive impact on the other, more traditional means of communicating.

Many of you may be able to relate to this scenario: I miss my daughter. I just want to hear her voice. Instinctively, I reach for the phone. After the usual "how are you, how is school" queries, I suddenly discover that, at the moment, I really don't have anything interesting to talk about.

I'm sure my daughter is perplexed about why dad is urgently calling her long distance to ask how she is doing in school. But, with a copy of the latest completed test nearby, I am able to quickly refer to her clever spin on The Big Green Rat from Outer Space, saving myself the embarrassment of a temporary mental shutdown.

The tests provides a wealth of subjects for discussion. Chatting about Dion's drawings and answers not only provides fuel for future questions, but also sets the stage for a continuing and meaningful dialogue.

However, you may discover that too much discussion with your child about his or her answers may disturb the safe shelter the tests provide. I've found that these questionnaires create a world of their own. Part of the magic of this world is the way that thoughts and ideas can be exchanged without a spoken word.

In the end, how you decide to act on what you've learned about yourself and your will be your decision. Perhaps there'll be much to do—dissecting the answers, analyzing the artwork, and discussing the "red flags." But it's also possible that there is nothing to be done, except to cherish and nurture the bond between you and your child, enhanced within the playful realm of the Dad's Tests. In short, it's the *fun* you share that may be the most important thing.

The Dad's Questions for Dion Test

Here it is, the test that started it all!

I have to chuckle when I look at this test today. I recall how excited I was about it at the time, but, compared to the "ultra-mod" grandeur of my current questionnaires, it seems so awkward and primitive. Still, it was a successful experiment, and I can see that I was locking into a process.

I also notice that I completely omitted question number 29. I wonder what that question might have been? Perhaps, on a future test, I should include two questions numbered 29 to make up for the slight!

All in all, I don't think it was really what I learned from this first test that was important. It was the rapport it initiated that was the magic for me!

However, without the test, I might never have been aware about her almost-spiritual reverence for pizza!

QUESTIONS, QUIRKS AND COMMENTS

QUESTION 10 *"How is your Mom?"*

A question like this might cause problems. Steer away from queries about other grown ups, especially parents. While your intentions might be innocent, they may be misunderstood by your child or the third party the question relates to.

QUESTION 14 *"Can you think of any new thing we could become famous for?"*

This question was based on another one of those on-going jokes between Dion and me. In the past, I had sent her letters in which I would ask her about silly things that we could get famous for. Her answer, *"Teach our dogs and cats to bark and meow Xmas songs,"* I thought was clever, and, who knows, might have worked!

QUESTION 27 *"What is your favorite animal?"*

This was really just a "filler" question. I expected her to just say "dog" or "cat." Her answer, *"Every animal,"* I thought, was very touching and really said something about my daughter as a person.

QUESTION 36 *"Do you know what you want to be when you grow up?"*

Her answer, *"A good-paid person,"* makes sense to me!

THE DAD'S QUESTIONS FOR DION TEST

OCT 1990

① HOW ARE YOU?
   NOT SO GOOD ___ OK ___ FINE ___ GREAT ✗

② DID YOU GET MY POST CARDS?
   YES ✗ NO ___

③ DID YOU GET ANY POST CARDS FROM SUSAN?
   YES ✗ ·NO ___

④ HOW WAS YOUR VACATION?
   NOT FUN ___ SO-SO ___ OK ___ FUN ___ GREAT ✗

⑤ HAVE YOU HAD ANY THUNDER STORMS SINCE I WAS there?
   YES ___ NO ✗

⑥ IF ANSWER WAS YES, WHAT WERE they like?
   NO BIG DEAL ___ FUN ___ SCARY ___ WAY COOL ___

⑦ HOW is TOBY?
   FINE ✗ DIRTY ✗ CRAZY ___ FINE, CRAZY AND DIRTY ✗

⑧ HOW is PEE-PEE?
   SWEET ___ CRAZY ___ PURRRRR-FECT ✗

⑨ HOW DO YOU LIKE SCHOOL?
   NOT MUCH ___ NOT AT ALL ___ it's OK ✗ love it ___ WISH YOU LIVED THERE

⑩ HOW is YOUR MOM?
   GOOD ___ TIRED ___ GOOD AND TIRED ✗ Wonderful AS Always ___

⑪ DO YOU STILL HAVE YOUR TURTLE?
   YES ___ NO ✗ RAN AWAY ✗ SET FREE ___ lost ___

⑫ HOW FAR CAN YOU GET IN MARIO I?
   WORLD? #8-4 SAVE PRINCESS ✗

⑬ WHAT ARE YOU GOING to BE ON HALLOWEEN?
   Don't KNOW YET ___ or Cleopatra ___

⑭ CAN YOU THINK OF ANY NEW THINGS WE COULD BECOME FAMOUS FOR?
   No ___ or teach our dogs cats to bark

⑮ HAVE YOU DONE ANY NEW DRAWINGS?
   meow to Christmas songs.
   YES ✗ No ___

⑯ IF ANSWER is YES, WILL YOU SEND ME ONE?
   YES ✗ No ___

⑰ ARE THERE ANY NEW PHOTOS OF YOU OR YOUR PETS?
YES ✗ NO ___

⑱ IF ANSWER IS YES, CAN YOU SEND ME ONE?
YES ✗ NO ___

⑲ DOES YOUR DAD LOVE YOU?
YES ✗ YES ☺ YES ♥♥♥

⑳ WHAT IS YOUR FAVORITE FOOD?
pizza

㉑ FAVORITE SNACK?
pizza

㉒ FAVORITE DRINK?
pizza ubI mean O.D.
Dr pepper

㉓ FAVORITE COLOR?
pinkepoo

㉔ WHO IS YOUR BEST FRIEND?
Jessica Crewe

㉕ FAVORITE TV OR MOVIE STAR?
Don't know

㉖ FAVORITE SINGER?
Don't know & DAD

㉗ FAVORITE ANIMAL?
Every animal

㉘ FAVORITE TOY?
DONT
KNOW

㉚ HOW TALL ARE YOU?
REAL TALL ___ NOT VERY ___ DON'T KNOW ✗ OR ___

㉛ DO YOU KNOW WHAT YOU WANT FOR X-MAS?   YES
NO ___ HAVEN'T THOUGHT ABOUT IT ___ OR ___

㉜ WHAT IS THE FUNNIEST WORD YOU KNOW? 00g a/og a

㉝ WHAT DO YOU HATE? pee wee ~~herman~~ HermenStrawberry short
cake

㉞ THERE WAS A little MAN IN CHINA TOWN: WHATS THE NEXT LINE?
He was a little man indeed

㉟ WHICH DO YOU LIKE BEST?
NIGHTTIME ___ DAYTIME ✗

㊱ DO YOU KNOW WHAT YOU WANT TO BE WHEN YOU GROW UP?
NOT SURE ✗ OR goodpayed person,

㊲ PLEASE WRITE YOUR NAME the best you CAN.........
Dionne K.

THE ALL NEW DAD'S QUESTIONS FOR DION TEST PART II

After the triumphant response to the first test, I was inspired to press ahead with great forti-.......................tude. Even the title demonstrated my energized conviction.

This mighty effort soared to a whopping 42 questions. This time I boldly included a number of boxes for drawings. To this day, I consider the drawings for Question 34 priceless treasures.

Since the very existence of Santa was falling into doubt, letters to the North Pole became a diminished priority. Questions 1 and 2 allowed me to swoop in on "Go-Go My Walking Pup" and "Baby Alive" with pinpoint accuracy, while cautiously avoiding "Liver" or "Dead Bugs," thanks to question 4.

QUESTIONS, QUIRKS AND COMMENTS

QUESTIONS 13 through 16 After I bought Dion her first Nintendo system, whenever she would see me, she wanted me to play video games with her. After a while, she got me hooked. By answering my questions and drawing a diagram, she was able to show me how to find the Warps in Mario 3. Quite a "long distance achievement, don't you think?

QUESTION 22 What a relief! I don't have to worry about boys—yet.

QUESTION 29 As I begin to establish my tradition of recurring themes, I once again inquired, *"Is there anything we could do on Halloween that we can become famous for?"* Her answer, *"Go with our animals and make people think they were kids in Halloween costumes,"* assured me that a bonanza of imagination was just waiting to be tapped.

QUESTION 32 When I asked, *"What is your favorite subject in school?"* I was startled by her answer, *"science."* It instantly conjured up visions of microscopes and test tubes as future birthday gifts.

QUESTION 36 This question falls into the "Ask a stupid question, get a stupid answer" category and provided me with my first lesson from Dion in "Dad-testing." When I'm asking for three things she has learned to cook, an answer like *"Breakfast, lunch and dinner"* should only be expected.

THE ALL NEW DAD'S QUESTIONS FOR DION TEST PART 2

① NAME two things you really, really, really...... really WANT FOR X-MAS
　　① Giant trampeline
　　② GOGO puppy

② NAME two things you really WANT FOR X-MAS
　　① Super MARio 2
　　② BABY ALiVE

③ NAME two things you KINDA' WANT FOR X-MAS
　　① N.W.K. dolls even though I hate the N.K.O.T.B.
　　② game boy, 'turtle

④ NAME two things you don't WANT FOR X-MAS
　　① Live or dead bug,
　　② Liver

⑤ HAVE YOU SEEN the NEW GiFTED CHILDREN'S CATALOGUE?
　　YES _____ No ☒

⑥ If YOUR ANSWER WAS YES, DiD you SEE ANYTHiNG YOU like that You did'nt list ABOVE?
　　YES _____ No _____ If YES, what? _____

⑦ WHAT DOES tOBY WANT FOR X-MAS?
　　DON'T KNOW _____ DiD'NT ASK _____ OR treats

⑧ WHAT DOES BUD WANT FOR X-MAS?
　　DON'T KNOW _____ HE DiD'NT SAY _____ OR treats and dog
　　closes.
⑨ WHAT DOES PEE-PEE WANT FOR X-MAS?
　　DON'T KNOW _____ PRE-FURRRRS NOT TO SAY _____ OR treats and toys

⑩ Do You think X-MAS trees should be DECORATED WITH PiECES OF PIZZA?
　　YES _____ No ☒ ALWAYS _____

⑪ Do You think the lAST QUESTiON WAS STUPiD?
　　YES ☒ No _____

⑫ HOW MANY HOURS HAVE YOU PLAYED MARIO Ⅲ SINCE YOU GOT IT ?
   NOT MANY _____ QUITE A FEW _____ MILLIONS _____ ZILLIONS _☆__

⑬ IN MARIO Ⅲ CAN YOU TELL ME WHICH WORLD OR WORLDS I CAN FIND WARPS IN
   WORLD ① GRASS LAND _☆__ WORLD ② DESERT LAND _☆__
   WORLD ③ WATER LAND _____ WORLD ④ GIANT LAND _____
   WORLD ⑤ SKY LAND _____ WORLD ⑥ ICE LAND _____
   WORLD ⑦ PIPELAND _____ WORLD ⑧ DARK LAND _____ NOT SURE _

⑭ IF THE FIRST WARP IS IN WORLD _1_ WHAT PART ON THE MAP IS IT ?
   PART ① ___ PART ② ___ PART ③ _☆ PART ④ ___ PART ⑤ ___ PART ⑥ ___
   PART ⑦ ___ PART ⑧ ___ PART ⑨ ___ PART ⑩ ___ NOT SURE _____

⑮ IF THE FIRST WARP IS IN WORLD _1_ PART _3_ , IS IT AT
   THE BEGINNING _____ IN THE MIDDLE _____ OR AT THE END _☆__ NOT SURE _

⑯ CAN YOU DRAW A PICTURE OF WHERE I SHOULD BE TO FIND THE WARP ?

⑰ CAN YOU TELL ME ANYTHING ELSE TO HELP ME FIND THE WARPS ?
   YES _____ NO _☆__ OR _____

(18) ARE YOU SICK OF ANSWERING QUESTIONS ABOUT MARIO AND the WARPS?

YES ____ NO ✗ CAN'T ANSWER BECAUSE YOU'RE SICK OF ANSWERING -

QUESTIONS ABOUT MARIO AND the WARPS ____

(19) ON YOUR lAST TEST YOU SAID YOUR TURTLE RANAWAY, WHERE DO YOU think HE WENT?

JUST OFF to hANG OUT WITH OTHER TURTLES ✗

To Hollywood to bECOME A MOVIE STAR ____

To SCHOOL To LEARN to bE A BRAIN Surgeon ____ OTHER ____

(20) WHICH DO YOU like bEST?

SUMMER ____ SPRING ____ WINTER ✗ FALL ✗

(21) WOULD YOU EVER WANT To GO INTO OUTER SPACE OR TO ANOTHER PLANET?

YES ✗ NO ____ DON'T KNOW ____ YOU AlREADY ARE ____

(22) WHAT DO YOU Think About boys

KINDA' like them ____ like them ____ LOVE them ____ HATE them ✗ DON'T KNOW ____

(23) WHAT IS YOUR FAVORITE GAME? MARIO 3, Life, Monoply, Clue, Mario2 Mario1.

(24) WHAT IS YOUR FAVORITE TV SHOW? Don't Know.

(25) IF YOU HAD TO BE TURNED INTO AN ANIMAL, WHAT WOULD YOU BE? ~~cat~~ Pee-Pee She's spoiled and still spoiling.

(26) WHAT IS THE BEST THING ABOUT DISNEYLAND? Rides and food everything eat

(27) SANTA CLAUS' FAVORITE X-MAS WAS the best est ONE OF ALL.

(28) WHAT CAT STARS IN the COMMERCIAL FOR Who's that Kitty CAT FOOD? Auhee

(29) IS there ANYTHING WE COULD DO ON HALLOWEEN that WE COULD bECOME FAMOUS FOR?

Go with our Animals and make people think the were kids in Halloween Costumes.

(30) DO you think you WOULD LIKE PIZZA ICE CREAM

YES ____ NO ✗ MAYBE ____

(31) WHY DID THE BABY SNAKE GO To SCHOOL?

DON'T KNOW ✗

To LEARN to READ SLITHER-A-TURE ____

To STUDY Hissssstory ✗

(32) WHAT IS YOUR FAVORITE SUbJECT IN school? Science

(33) DO YOU like the DAD'S QUESTIONS FOR DION TESTS   YES ✗ ____ NO ____

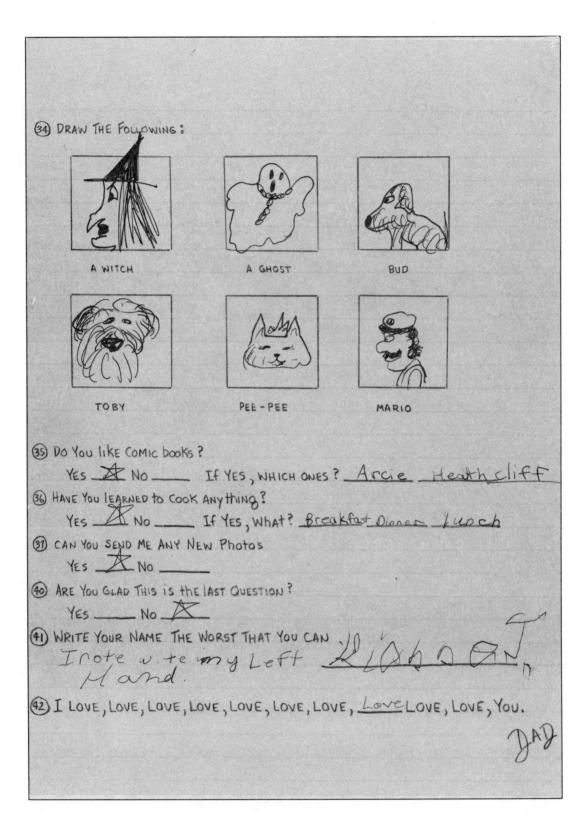

34 DRAW THE FOLLOWING:

A WITCH

A GHOST

BUD

TOBY

PEE-PEE

MARIO

35 DO YOU LIKE COMIC BOOKS?
YES ✗ NO ___ IF YES, WHICH ONES? _Arcie_ _Heathcliff_

36 HAVE YOU LEARNED TO COOK ANYTHING?
YES ✗ NO ___ IF YES, WHAT? _Breakfast Dinner Lunch_

37 CAN YOU SEND ME ANY NEW PHOTOS
YES ✗ NO ___

40 ARE YOU GLAD THIS IS THE LAST QUESTION?
YES ___ NO ✗

41 WRITE YOUR NAME THE WORST THAT YOU CAN
I rote w. te my Left _ZiAhoaJ,_
Hand.

42 I LOVE, LOVE, LOVE, LOVE, LOVE, LOVE, LOVE, _Love_ LOVE, LOVE, YOU.

DAD

THE ALL NEW BIGGER & BETTER THAN EVER
1991 DAD'S QUESTIONS FOR DION TEST: THE NEXT GENERATION

Since my travels in 1991 allowed me to visit Dion on a few occasions, and I knew her life was ....somewhat disrupted by her move from Oklahoma to Arkansas, it wasn't until the early fall that this next installment of the Dad's Test was completed.

I guess the fact that Dion had moved even further away and so much time had elapsed since the previous test accounts for the "Dead Sea Scroll" length of this questionnaire. I had a lot of questions about her new living conditions and how she was making the adjustment.

Perhaps this test should have been called "Dad Gets Strung Out On Cappucino For Dion Test." It was, however, the first test to feature a cover with original art, which I thought was a nice touch.

Along with early Christmas inquiries, I added lots of requests for drawings, which yielded the awesome "Alien From Mars." Steven Spielberg, eat your heart out!

It was also interesting to learn about her fascination with science was continuing and that she was already thinking of college . . . whoa!

QUESTIONS, QUIRKS AND COMMENTS

QUESTION 23 I decided to make further queries to find

out if she liked to eat anything besides pizza. Can you imagine my horror when *"barbeque"* appeared on her list of *"What do you hate the most?"* I wondered if there might have been a mix-up in the maternity ward!

QUESTION 42 My request for a short poem was granted. However, I found it illuminating that she had clearly labeled her effort "a song." I realized it was a little early to be calling her a chip off the old block, but I liked the way she was thinking.

QUESTION 53 *"Do you ever go to church or Sunday school?"* I was pleased to learn that she was already attending church twice a week.

QUESTION 63 Once again I try to assess her culinary skills. *"If you had to cook a dinner, what could you do best?"* Her answer: *"Food."* At this point, I know she's trying to play Tic Tac Toe with dad's brain.

QUESTION 87 The fact that she could only name two of my four brothers could have seemed disturbing, but the question lets her know that I have four brothers. It's a beginning. Use questions like this to acquaint your child with relatives he or she may be unaware of or has forgotten.

QUESTION 88 *"Would you ever like to come live with your dad for a while?"* At the time, this question seemed harmless to me, but it really wasn't. What am I expecting her to do—make a choice she doesn't really have? It's hard enough being a child without this needless weight. Avoid questions like this altogether.

QUESTION 98 *"What do you wish someone would invent?"* Her response: *"One day per year schooling."* Edison would have been impressed!

THE ALL NEW, BIGGER AND BETTER THAN EVER 1991 DAD'S Questions FOR DioN Test: the Next Generation

① How ARE You? NOT Good ____ OK ____ CHINE ____ GREAT ✓

If ANSWER was NOT Good, why? _____

② Do You like LIVING IN ARKANSAS? No ____ YES ✓

If ANSWER is No, why _____

③ Do You MISS TULSA? YES ____ No ✓ Just A little ____

④ Do You MISS YOUR FRIENDS IN TULSA? YES ✓ No ____

⑤ How do you like YOUR NEW SCHOOL? HATE it ____ Love it ✓

About the SAME AS TULSA *NO*

If ANSWER is HATE it, why? _____

⑥ HAVE YOU MADE ANY NEW FRIENDS? YES ✓ No ____

⑦ How MANY? ____ ALOT ✓

⑧ If ANSWER to ⑥ is YES, WHAT ARE SOME OF THEIR NAMES? note
Carrie Hyde, Crystal Alison, Ande   Ande is girl

⑨ How MANY PEOPLE LIVE IN the HOUSE you live IN? 2

⑩ How MANY PETS? 4

⑪ NAME three things you MIGHT WANT TO BE, when you grow up?
① Singer
② Artist, actor
③ Something famous, or pays good

⑫ NAME three things you WOULD NEVER WANT TO BE
① Bergan
② Undertaker
③ Bugger

⑬ What is your FAVORITE TV show? Well here one is Saterday Night Live

⑭ FAVORITE SONG? Hard Vanig Ice, McHamnner songs Pop, I can't say one song

⑮ THREE FAVORITE MOVIES? ① Anone of the Gables
② Cry Baby
③ Disney Movies

16. NAME ALL THE VIDEO GAMES YOU HAVE. SuperM., S.Mario2 and 3, Monter Party, Chiller, Disneys Majic Kingdom.

17. ARE THERE ANY YOU WISH YOU HAD? Yes., Donkey Kong, Tetres, Antispatatio, Monoply, and ect.

18. WHAT SIZE SHOE DO YOU WEAR? 6½ womens

19. WHAT SIZE SHIRT DO YOU WEAR? 14,

20. HOW TALL ARE YOU? 4ft 8inches

21. HOW MANY FRECKLES ARE ON YOUR NOSE? too many

22. WHAT IS YOUR FAVORITE? NAME EACH OF THE FOLLOWING:

FAV-① CANDY toffee things

FAV-② DESERT cheese cake

FAV-③ SNACK chips, nut, ect,

FAV-④ DRINK DR. Pepper, water

FAV-⑤ FRUIT peach

FAV-⑥ VEGETABLE corn, ockra

FAV-⑦ DINNER macaronie, pizza, c.burges, chicken, steak, ect.

23. WHAT DO YOU HATE THE MOST? NAME EACH OF THE FOLLOWING:

HATE ① CANDY real real sweet camoly

HATE ② DESERT chocolate cake with choco iceing fudge shewings

HATE ③ SNACK choco covered raslans

HATE ④ DRINK Grape fruit juice

HATE ⑤ FRUIT apples, or venens

HATE ⑥ VEGETABLE spinich of course

HATE ⑦ DINNER Barbecue,

24. DO YOU STILL HAVE YOUR ART BOX? YES ✓ NO

25. IS YOUR NINTENDO SYSTEM SET UP? YES ✓ NO

26. HOW MANY HOURS A WEEK DO YOU PLAY? ?

㉗ Do you still have your JEWELRY BOX? YES ✓ No ____

㉘ What is your FAVORITE DAY of the Week? _Friday, silly_

Month. _December_

SEASON: Winter ✓ Spring ____ Summer ____ FALL ✓

㉙ NAME three things you really, really, really WANT FOR X-MAS

① _video games_

② _mini T.V. (I won't get this one for a while)_

③ _VHS tapes (Garfield, fairy tales, Disney)_

㉚ NAME THREE things you would really LIKE FOR X-MAS

① _Board games_

② _Dolls, Martha? la but yes more_

③ _Chandler Q_

㉛ WRITE YOUR FULL NAME BACKWARDS _yelliuT, lireAcnnoiD_ ^AAAA

㉜ NAME three things you KINDA' WANT FOR X-MAS

① _A car, just kidding, a stuffed animal_

② _cook book_

③ _Don't know yet._

㉝ MARK THREE FAVORITE Holidays, NOT COUNTING X-MAS PUT A STAR ON YOUR FAVORITE

✗ VALENTINES DAY ✓   ✱ 4th of JULY | Elemination
   EASTER   ✱ HALLOWEEN | Prosses
   ~~GROUND HOG DAY~~   ~~THANKSGIVING~~
   ~~NEW YEARS DAY~~   ~~St. PATRICKS DAY~~
   ~~April Fools DAY~~   ~~Columbus DAY~~
   ~~WASHINGTON'S BIRTHDAY~~   ~~LABOR DAY~~

㉞ What is your FAVORITE color? _Purple, Black gold,_

㉟ Do You hAVE your OWN ROOM? YES ✓ No ____

If No, who do you shARE with? ____

㊱ DOES MR. RAT GO OUT FOR A CORN DOG? YES ✓ No ____

(37) HAVE YOU SAVED the letters AND POSTCARDS I'VE SENT YOU THROUGH THE YEARS? YES ✓ NO ___ A FEW ___ ALOT ___

(38) Without ASK^ING^ YOUR MOM, CAN YOU spell MY MIDDLE NAME? I'll try/Allen Alan

(39) Who is the only Living relATIVE of JULIO MANGLES AND HEIR TO the MANGLES FORTUNE? Dianne Twilley

(40) ABOUT WHAT TIME DO YOU GO TO BED? SCHOOL DAYS 11:00 WEEKENDS As long as I want

(41) ABOUT WHAT TIME DO YOU GET UP? SCHOOL DAYS 7:__ WEEKENDS never 12:00

(42) WRITE A short POEM ABOUT TOBY. On Toby's Rossision

I wish I had a sandwich, an icecream one prefered,
I never werepants, I like to breakdance so you can't
call me a nerd.

a song.

(43) If you hAD to bE AN ANIMAL, WHAT WOULD YOU BE? my cat

(44) WHAT IS YOUR FAVORITE SUBJECT IN SCHOOL? science

(45) WITHOUT ASKING YOUR MOM, HOW OLD IS YOUR DAD? 30 something
AND what is His BIRTHDAY? DAY ? Month ? YEAR ?

(46) THERE WAS A little MAN IN China TOWN

(47) What is tHE SCARIEST THING YOU CAN THINK OF? a ghost of a madmen

(48) What MAKES you the MOST HAPPY? toys nature animals

(49) What MAKES you the MOST SAD? road kill

(50) If You hAD one WISH? infinity wishes

(51) WHAT IS YOUR FAVORITE Book? Jungle Book

(52) Do You think People IN ARKANSAS TALK Differently? YES ✓ No ___

(53) Do YOU EVER GO TO CHURCH OR SUNDAY SCHOOL? YES ✓ NO ___
if YES, How ofTEN? ~~ONCE~~ Twice A WEEK ✓ A MONTH ___ A YEAR ___

(54) HOW MANY LEGS DOES MAX DOG HAVE? 0 zip

(55) WHO IS YOU'RE FAVORITE CARTOON CHARACTER? Garfied

(56) Do YOU THINK YOUR DOING WELL ON this TEST SO FAR? YES ✓ NO ___

(51) Find a Photograph of you. As best you can, draw a picture of your face.

(58) Do you have any money saved? Yes ___ ✓No ___ if Yes, How Much! -10

(59) Do you have a warm coat for winter? Yes ✓No ___
If Yes, Do you like it? Yes ✓No ___

(60) Have you saved the princess in Mario I yet? Yes ___ No ✓

(61) What is the furthest you have got in Mario III? 8 -1

(62) Do you like your Game? More than Regular Nintendo the same
About the Same ✓ Not as Much ___ Don't like it Anymore ___
BOY

(63) If you had to cook a dinner, What could you do Best? Food

(64) Would you like to learn to drive a car? Yes ✓ No ___ Not Yet ___
I sorta have

(65) Draw the house where you live.

66) Do you buy LUNCH AT SCHOOL? YES _____ or TAKE YOUR LUNCH? ✓

67) Do you have A CASSETTE PLAYER? YES ✓ No _____ OLD ONE ✓

68) CAN YOU NAME ALL SIX OF YOUR DAD's ALBUMS? Probly Not

    ① Wild dogs   ④
    ② Stubratimes   ⑤
    ③   ⑥

69) Do you HAVE ALL SIX OF MY ALBUMS? YES _____ No ✓ How MANY? 4

70) Who do you like best? ELVIS ✓ THE BEATLES _____

71) When it is 3 o'clock IN THE AFTERNOON IN ARKANSAS, What time is it in CALIFORNIA? _____ ? _____

72) Do you still have your MICROSCOPE? YES ✓ No _____
if yes, Do you ever use it? A little ✓ Not MUCH _____ NEVER _____

73) What KINDA' FOOD Do you Feed YOUR KITTY? Whiskas, Friskees
TOBY $ BUD Shurfine gravy and gravy train

74) Which Do You like best, TAKING A SHOWER ✓ OR A BATH? _____

75) TRY to COPY MY SIGNATURE.

76) WRITE YOUR OWN SIGNATURE.

77) Do you think there IS LIFE ON OTHER PLANETS?
YES _____ No _____ MAYbE ✓

78) Is There ANY SPORT You like to play? No Hardly

79) ANY SPORT You like to WATCH? no

80) What is Your FAVORITE Flower? Rose I guess

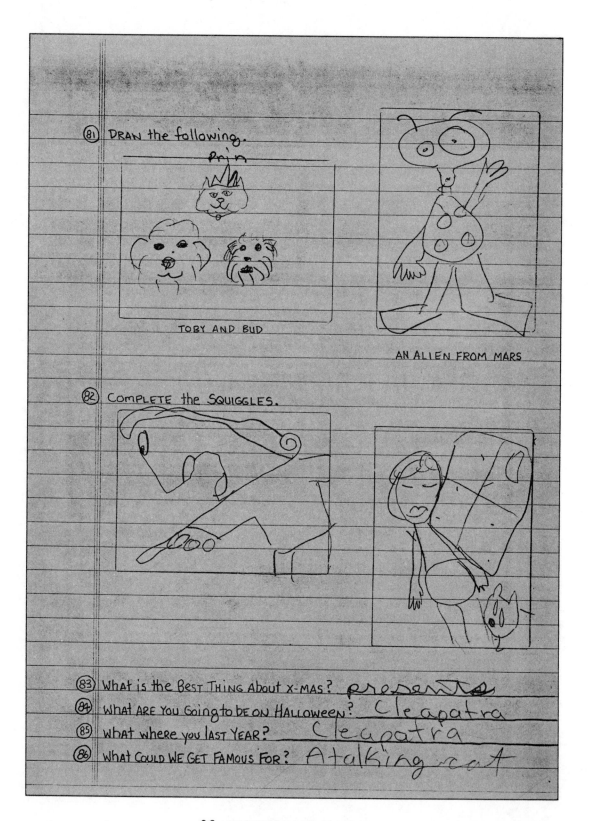

81) DRAN the following.

prin

TOBY AND BUD

AN ALIEN FROM MARS

82) COMPLETE the SQUIGGLES.

83) What is the BEST THING About X-MAS? presents

84) WHAT ARE YOU Going to BE ON HALLOWEEN? Cleapatra

85) WHAT where you LAST YEAR? Cleapatra

86) WHAT COULD WE GET FAMOUS FOR? A talking cat

87) I have four brothers. They are your uncles. Can you name them?
DWANE _____ _____ Dale

88) Would you ever like to come live with your Dad for a while?
YES___ No___ I don't know ✓

89) Do you like TV Dinners? YES ✓ No___
If Yes, what kind? chicken noodle

90) Do you like puzzles? YES ✓ No___ Not much___

91) Which Do you like best? A lightening storm ✓ ?
A SNOW STORM___ NEITHER___

92) Do you think you would ever like to learn to play a
muisical instrument? YES ✓ No
If yes, Do You know which one? No
If No, why not? _____

93) If you had a time Machine, where would you Go? Dinisaur
age

94) Name things you collect. erasers, pencils, pens,
stamps, avon, stuffed animals ect,

95) What do you hope Nobody will get you for X-mas? socks

96) Is there one place in the world you would really
like to go to someday? Austrialia

97) A place you would never want to go to New York

98) What do you wish someone would invent? 1 day per
a year schooling

99) Do you have your own scrap book? YES ✓ No___

100) How many stuffed Animals Do you have, Not Counting
About 30 I keep for you? 100 — 75 serisally

101) Do you like star trek? YES ✓ No___ the New one ✓
the old one ✓ the Movies ✓

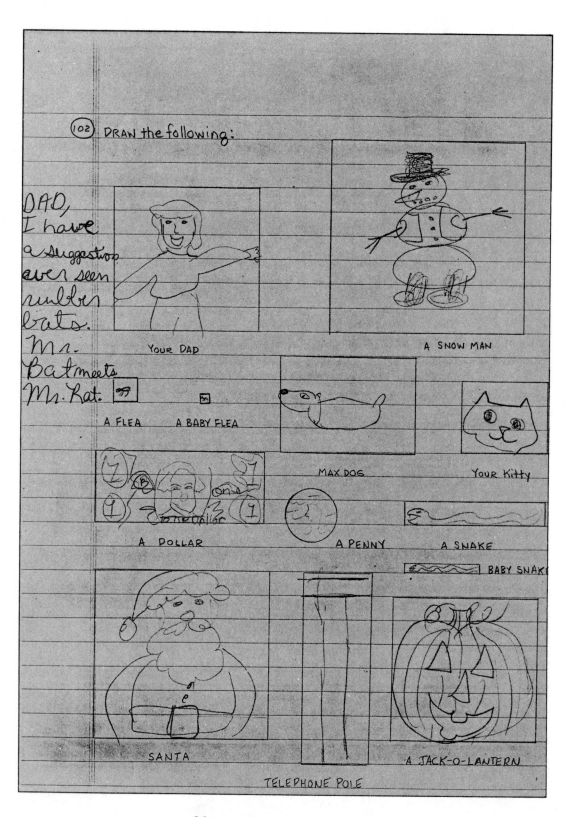

102 DRAW the following:

YOUR DAD

A SNOW MAN

DAD, I have a suggestion ever seen rubber bats. Mr. Bat meets Mr. Rat.

A FLEA   A BABY FLEA

MAX DOG

YOUR KITTY

A DOLLAR

A PENNY

A SNAKE

BABY SNAKE

SANTA

TELEPHONE POLE

A JACK-O-LANTERN

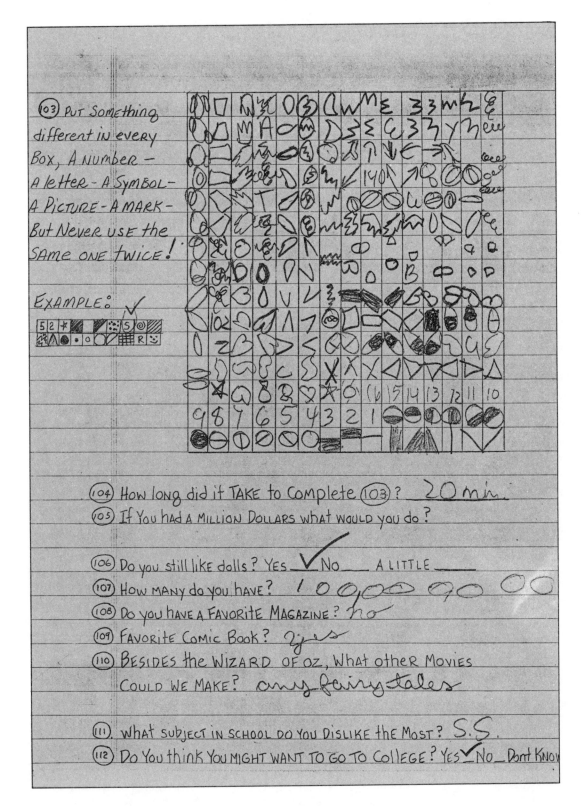

(103) Put something different in every box, a number — a letter — a symbol — a picture — a mark — But never use the same one twice!

EXAMPLE:

(104) How long did it TAKE to complete (103)? 20 min.

(105) If you had a million dollars what would you do?

(106) Do you still like dolls? YES ✓ No ___ A LITTLE ___

(107) How many do you have? 1 0 0 ○ ○ 9 0 ○ ○

(108) Do you have a favorite magazine? no

(109) Favorite Comic Book? yes

(110) Besides the Wizard of Oz, What other movies Could we make? any fairy-tales

(111) What subject in school do you dislike the most? S.S.

(112) Do you think you might want to go to college? YES ✓ No ___ Don't Know ___

(113) If you have any QUESTIONS about the test OR JUST WANT TO TALK You CAN CALL ANY DAY AFTER 4:00 PM FOR FREE. THE CORRECT NUMBER TO CALL IS? 1-800-555-1798 _____ OR 1-800-555-1798 ✓

(114) Your address in ARKANSAS is Route 12 Box 154. Sometimes Box Numbers will NOT Accept LARGE PACKAGES. FIND out if it is OK FOR ME to SEND YOUR PACKAGES to this Address? YES: _____ No ✓
If No, What Address should I MAIL IT TO?   Ramonds Thrift way

(115) I, L O V E L O V E L O V E L O V E L O V E You.

(116) Do think this test was better than the LAST ONE?   Cazy
YES ✓ No _____ About the SAME _____

(117) Are you looking FORWARD to the NEXT ONE?
YES ✓ No _____ Not FOR A while _____ NOT FOR A LONG WHILE _____

(118) What TOY have you had the longest TIME, BUT STILL Like?
?   I'm not sure what all I have

(119) MAKE A X-MAS CARD, ANY KIND, ANY COLOR PAPER. CUT IT OUT AND TAPE OR PASTE IT IN THE BOX MARKED ON the INSIDE of this TABLET.

(120) MAKE A HALLOWEEN CARD. PLACE it ON the back of this TABLET.

(121) ARE YOU GLAD this TEST IS ALMOST OVER? YES _____ No ✓

(122) THROUGHOUT the TEST, which of your drawings turned out best? ?

(123) Do you have a bicycle? YES ✓ No _____ Would you like ONE? a new one

(125) Will You SEND ME Another Letter Sometime SOON? I'll try yes

(126) FOR A Million Dollars, would you Kill A Rabbit?   no

(127) CAN you GIVE ME A pretty Good GUESS, About how long It took you to FINISH THE WHOLE TEST? hours

THE AFTER XMAS DAD'S QUESTIONS FOR DION TEST 1992

This is the first test where I finally leveled out to an even 100 questions. As you can see, the eager reception of dad's exams continued undaunted, as evidenced by my daughter's message, "PLEASE SEND ME MORE," urgently scribed on the first page.

The title art was probably one of my worst efforts. Instead of "After Christmas," it looks more like "During Halloween." What a mistake! Why didn't I use a cover, like I did on the last test? When I got the test back and placed it along side the previous tests, I vowed that all my questionnaires would have covers from that point on. Sloppiness aside, this quiz is one of my favorites.

This edition features a truly excellent rendering of "Samster the Hamster" in Question 29, an invaluable insight into the sacred law, "Thou shalt not withhold little plastic animals from thy child at Christmas."

A few more serious issues are sandwiched between the Little Bunny Family and the Teenage Mutant Ninja Hamsters. A splendid time is guaranteed for all!

QUESTIONS, QUIRKS AND COMMENTS

QUESTION 23 This question earned one of my favorite responses from Dion: *"Did you feel sad about home-*

less people at Christmas?" Her reply, *"I forgot this year,"* I thought was a very honest and candid answer. For some reason, I know I'll never forget it. There are enough sad things in the world for a little girl to think about at Christmas. I think it's okay she forgot this one.

QUESTIONS 69 and 70 These questions address a scary issue I knew I eventually had to face. I'm also sure I could have easily bumbled the whole thing over the phone. Fortunately, I felt pretty good about the results. In Question 69, I ask *"Do you know any kids that use drugs?"* Her affirmative response was enough to sober even a former hippie like myself. Question 70 inquires, *"Using drugs is: OK; OK if you're careful; OK to try once or twice; Stupid and might kill you."* I believe her "check" on the last answer was honest and allowed dad to sleep much better. I strongly suggest you try the exact same question, or something very similar.

QUESTIONS 73 and 89 Questions like *"The Dad's tests are: Too long; Too short; about right,"* or *"Are you glad this test is almost over?"* are a good way to gauge your success as a "dad-tester." If you receive a disappointing response, perhaps it's time for a visit from the Flea Family.

THE AFTER
X-MAS
DAD'S QUESTIONS TEST
FOR DION
1992

Please send me more

① How was your X-mas? OK ____ FINE X GREAT ____

② Was your X-mas, Better than last year ____ About the same X

③ Did it snow? Yes ____ No X

④ Do you wish X-mas came twice a year? Yes X No ____

⑤ Name your 3 Favorite Big Presents.
  ① *T.V.*
  ② *Areil Doll*
  ③ *~~I don't know~~ cards*

⑥ Name your 3 Favorite Little Presents.
  ① *stamp*
  ② *dolphin ring*
  ③ *stuff*

⑦ What present was the biggest surprise? *That's a hard ?*

⑧ Did you get anything you didn't like? Yes ____ No ~~~~
  If yes, what?

⑨ Did you get 2 of the same thing? Yes ____ No ~~~~
  If yes, what?

QUESTIONS FROM DAD **95**

10 Try to LIST 30 things you got FOR X-MAS, No MATTER HOW SMALL, MORE if you CAN.

mermaid

① ~~pen~~
② Mermaid ~~Ball~~ & Dress
③ Dresses and exeseries
④ Prince Eric
⑤ T.V.
⑥ phone
⑦ radio

Garfield

⑧ alarm clock
⑨ Odie ~~& animal~~
⑩ back scrubber
⑪ toothbrust holder

Mermaid

⑫ Bangles
⑬ toothbrush ✓
⑭ paste
⑮ bubblebath

⑯ Monoldy
⑰ Antiscapation
⑱ Tetras
⑲ Mario set
⑳ Bunny set
㉑ ~~Snoopy~~
㉒ Fantasia
㉓ Peter Pan
㉔ Ja
㉕ pe
㉖ 5
㉗ ring
㉘ pound puppy
㉙ ~~avon~~
㉚ ~~clothes~~

Nin.

I cant think of anything els right now

11 Which GAME Do you like the best?
① TETRIS _____
② ~~MONOPOLY~~ _____
③ ~~ANTICIPATION~~ _____
④ DON'T KNOW yet ✗

12 HAVE you SEEN FANTASIA BEFORE? YES ✓ No ___

13 Do you like it? No ___ Alittle ___ ALOT ___ LOVE it ✓

⑭ How many days before X-MAS did you get the box I sent? _____ 2

⑮ Did you open it the day you got it? the box, box

⑯ Which 3 kinds of trading cards did you like best?

① Wizard of Oz

② Disney

③ Bill & Ted

⑰ If I find other kinds of trading cards, would you want me
to get them for you? Yes _____ No _____

⑱ Have you ever seen cards like these before? Yes _____ No _____

⑲ Are there any kinds of cards that I sent you that you   well some
would like more of? Yes _____ No _____
If yes, which ones? _____ ones I like
or other neat ones

⑳ Did you like my new X-MAS songs? Yes ● No _____ Kinda _____ Alot _____

㉑ Which one did you like the best?

X-MAS NIGHT _____

X-MAS LOVE _____

Both _____

Don't Know _____

㉒ Can you think of a name of a X-MAS song I could write?

_____

㉓ Did you feel sad about homeless people at X-MAS?   Forgot
Yes _____ No _____ Did'nt think about it _____   this year

㉔ Did your pets get anything for X-MAS? Yes _____ No _____
If yes, what?
Bud Candy cane toys
Toby bones
Princess toys

25) WHAT IS YOUR turtle's NAME? _Godzilla_

26) WHAT IS YOUR hamster's NAME? _Tony, I call him Barnaster Hamster_

27) WHAT ARE YOUR ducks' NAMES?

① _Beatoven_

② _Mohoh_

28)

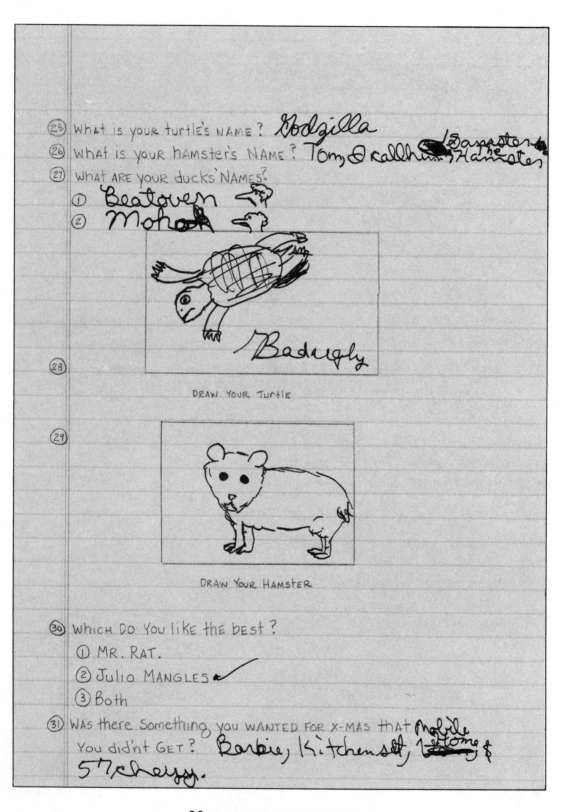

Badugly

DRAW YOUR Turtle

29)

DRAW YOUR HAMSTER

30) WHICH DO YOU like the best?

① MR. RAT.

② Julio MANGLES ✓

③ Both

31) WAS there Something you WANTED FOR X-MAS that _Mobile_
You did'nt GET? _Barbie, Kitchenset, Tony &
5 cherry._

(32) SINCE you don't like sports AND I don't like sports,
DID you think it WAS strange that I Sent You "ANGELS
IN the OUTFIELD? YES ✓ No _____

(33) HAVE You seen it Before? YES _____ No ✓

(34) DID You like it? YES _____ No _____ KINDA' _____ AloT _____ LOVED it _____
HAVEN'T WATCHED it YET _____

(35) If your PETS WROTE you A letter like the ONE MoM WROTE
To ME WHAT is ONE thing TOBY MIGHT SAY? 🐾
Get him to write one.

(36) WHAT MIGHT BUD SAY?
ditto

(37) WHAT WOULD PRINCESS SAY?
ditto

(38) WHAT WOULD YOUR TURTLE SAY?
O

(39) WHAT WOULD YOUR HAMSTER SAY?
|

(40) WHAT WOULD your ducks SAY?
++o

(41) DO YOU WISH I HADN'T SPENT SO MUCH MONEY on the MINI TV
AND GOT YOU MORE toys instead? I don't know

42) ARE You Going to use the picture cup I sent You or Just SAVE it?
use it ____ SAVE it ✓ throw it AWAY ____ Put things in it ____
use it FoR shaving ____ Don't KNow ____ other ____

43) Where is the little bunny FAMILY Going to live? *on the shelf next to my kitty tins*

44) WHat does to *←* FROM *←* MEAN?
Baby, Daddy, snake

45) Do you think DADS should be SAD if they don't get A
CARD or A gift FRom their child AT X-MAS? YES ✓ No ____

46) Do you wish I would Quit sending you those silly
PLASTIC ANimALS EVERY YEAR? YES ____ No ✓

47) Do you think CARRIE (THE Puppy) is CUTE? YES ✓ No ____

48) Did you think her Adventure in the TENT WAS FUNNY? *yes*

49) Do you think CARRIE AND Mow did A good Job WRAPPING youR X-MAS
Gifts? YES ✓ No ____ BUD AND PRINCESS could do Better ____

50) Do you think youR teAchers will believe youR mini TV is A
LUNCH Box? YES ____ No ✓ oh dad ____

51) Do you wish you HAd A baby brother or sister? YES ____ No ✓

52) Which would you RATHER HAVE? BRother ____ Sister ✓

53) When you get youR presents FRom SUSAN AND JAMIE, will you
CAll oR Write them AND SAy thank you? YES ✓ No ____

54) HAD you ever played the Monopoly VIDEO GAME beFoRe I
got it FoR you? YES ____ No ✓

55) WHat is the WoRst NAME FoR A GIRL? *Gritchen, Mildred*

56) WHat is the WoRst NAME FoR A Boy? *Bubba Heath Seth Shane tt.*

57) Is there A TAco Bell IN ARKANSAS? YES ____ No ____

58) *There was a* LITTLE *man in* CHINA *town*

cornnuts mix

59. What do you feed your hamster? *[drawing]*

60. What size shoe does your turtle wear? *O*

61. Do you let anyone else see these tests I send you? *[scribble]*
    YES ___ No ___ Just Mom *✓* Friends ___ *not always at all*

62.
    DRAW
    YOUR
    DUCKS

63. Do the Video Tapes I sent you play OK on your VCR? YES *✓* No ___

64. What one word best describes my Halloween video? *weird*

65. What is your hamster's favorite TV show? *Micky Mouse*

66. Do you like country Western Music? Yes ___ No *✓* Don't know ___

67. Do you like the old black & white Sherlock Holmes Movies? *never been*

68. Do you like chili Dogs? Yes ___ No *X* Sometimes ___ Never ___
    Like chili and hot dogs, but not together *yep*

69. Do you know any kids that use Drugs? Yes *X* No

70. Using Drugs is: OK ___ OK if your careful ___
    OK, to try once or twice ___ Stupid and Might kill you *X*

71. Do you remember the Robot show I used to do for you & Susan? *yes*

72. Would that make a good video? *yes* ✓

73. The Dad's tests are: Too long ___ Too short *✓* About Right ___

74. What is the best you have done on Dr. Mario? *level 13 or so*

75. Are you looking forward to getting older? Yes ___ No *[scribble]*

75) Which do you think WOULD BE the BEST MOVIE? "Robo Duck" _____
"TEENAGE MUTANT NINJA HAMSTERS" X "FRANKENSTIEN'S Kitty, Lonzo" _____

76) Do you believe in GHOSTS? YES ✓ No _____ Don't KNOW _____

77) WhAT Do You think is A good NAME FOR A MOVIE? Buddy the Giant Pup

78) What Could WE GET FAMOUS FOR? making another movie

79) Did you like Mow's letter? YES ✓ No _____

80) CAN Your Kitty Type? YES ✓ No _____ she plays great PIANO too ✓

81) Did you think 1991 WAS A good YEAR? YES ✓ No _____

82) Will 1992 be BETTER? YES _____ No _____ Don't KNOW _____ Hope So ✓ !

83) How MANY days WERE you SICK OVER the Holidays? week or so

84) ARE you bACK to your SPUNKY SELF? YES _____ No _____ ALMOST ✓

85) Is there ANYthing you hope to do this YEAR?

86) ◎※#✳ ⌘÷○✳ ≡≤%ˣ? YES _____ No _____ ≡≸≠:○ _____ %⅗ _____ Don't KNOW ✓

87) IN MARIO III, the Most LIVES you CAN GET is 99 TRUE ✓ FALSE _____

88) Could you send me a Picture of your ducks? yes

89) ARE You GLAD this test is ALMOST OVER? YES _____ No ✓

90) WhAT is your FAVORITE FLAVOR ICE CREAM? Cholate

91) Do you think Julio MANGLES hAS EVER bEEN to ARKANSAS? maybe

92) Do you think I REPEAT SOME of MY QUESTIONS? YES _____ No ✓

93) Do you think I REPEAT SOME of MY QUESTIONS? YES ✓ No _____

94) How MANY AVON iTEMS ARE in your Collection? about 100

95) ARE You PLANNING to get ANY NEW pets? If YES, what? mabe cow, lamb, chickens, geese

96) HAVE You WON A GAME of MONOPOLY YET? YES ✓ No _____ ALMOST _____

97) Which ToKEN Do you use? car, horse, dog

98) Do You still hAVE A copy of Super Dion? on Beta

99) How long did it tAKE you to finish this test? I don't know

100) Your DAD, thinks your OK _____ KINDA likes you _____
LOVES you _____ LoVE, LoVES you _____ LOVE, LOVE, LOVE, LOVE,
LOVE, LOVE, LOVE, LOVE, LOVE, LOVE, LOVE, LOVE, LOVE, LOVES you ✓

100 Questions
From Dad

In this landmark decision, I have finally customized my title into the current "100 Questions From Dad" model.

Even my cover was a showroom centerpiece compared to the ugliness of Christmas past. Inside, a shaky "dot-to-dot" is saved by the sublimely captured essence of "Old Grandpa Snake."

The interactive atmosphere of the questionnaire continues to chart unpredictable paths. I ask Dion to *"Complete the squiggle."* She throws the ball back in my court, and requests that I complete *her* squiggle. I guess it's only fair.

QUESTIONS, QUIRKS AND COMMENTS

QUESTION 30 I was curious if, like when I was in school, there was one teacher Dion just hated. I was pleased that she confided in me and named the teacher. However, I've rendered the name illegible to protect the innocent.

QUESTION 31 In another school-related question, I probed, *"What is Samster's favorite subject?"* I received a choice response, *"Reading. He hates sci-ence-sometimes his cousins are used."* Good answer, Groucho!

QUESTION 38 I believe this is an important question for distant dads to ask: *"If anyone ever really hurt you or did something bad to you, would you tell your Dad?"* Not only does the question let your child know that you are concerned about how he or she is treated, it also initiates the idea that it would be okay to confide in dad if any problem arose.

QUESTION 63 Here's an example of how a simple question can turn out to be important. I thought she surely she knew my phone number! She didn't.

QUESTION 98 *"Could you call me sometime soon?"* Naturally a question like this will only fly if phone calls to and from your child are not a custodial issue.

100 QUESTIONS

FROM DAD

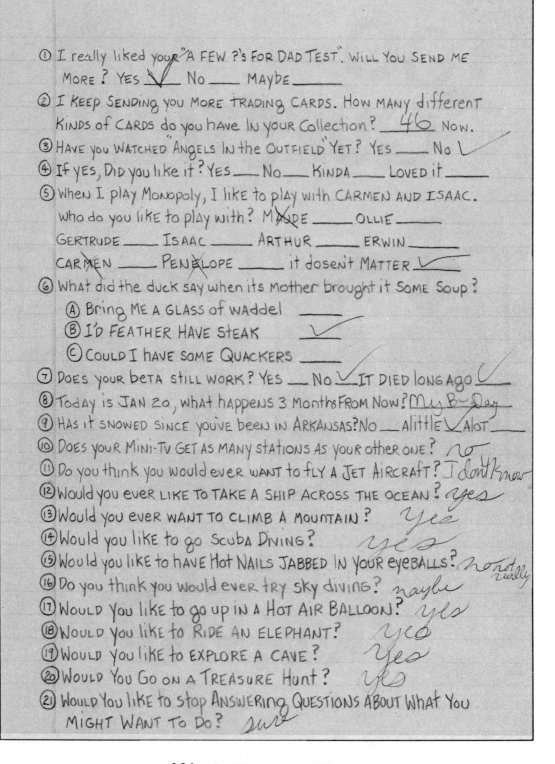

① I really liked your "A FEW ?'s FOR DAD TEST". WILL YOU SEND ME MORE? YES ✓ No ____ MAYbE ____

② I KEEP SENDING you MORE TRADING CARDS. How MANY different KINDS of CARDS do you have IN your Collection? __46__ Now.

③ HAVE you WATCHED "ANGELS IN the OUTFIELD" YET? YES ____ No ✓

④ If YES, DID you like it? YES ____ No ____ KINDA ____ LOVED it ____

⑤ When I play Monopoly, I like to play with CARMEN AND ISAAC. who do you like to play with? MAUDE ____ OLLIE ____ GERTRUDE ____ ISAAC ____ ARTHUR ____ ERWIN ____ CARMEN ____ PENELOPE ____ it dosen't MATTER ✓

⑥ What did the duck say when its mother brought it SOME Soup?
  Ⓐ Bring ME A GLASS of WADDEL ____
  Ⓑ I'D FEATHER HAVE STEAK ✓
  Ⓒ COULD I have SOME QUACKERS ____

⑦ DOES your beta still WORK? YES ____ No ✓ IT DIED long ago ✓

⑧ Today is JAN 20, what happens 3 MonthS FROM Now? My B-Day

⑨ HAS it SNOWED SINCE you've been IN ARKANSAS? No ____ A little ✓ Alot ____

⑩ DOES your MINI-TV GET AS MANY STATIONS AS your other ONE? no

⑪ Do you think you would ever WANT to FLY A JET AirCRAFT? I don't know

⑫ Would you ever LIKE TO TAKE A SHIP ACROSS THE OCEAN? yes

⑬ Would you ever WANT TO CLIMB A MOUNTAIN? Yes

⑭ Would you like to go SCUBA DIVING? yes

⑮ Would you like to have Hot NAILS JABBED IN YOUR eyeBALLS? no not really

⑯ Do you think you would ever try sky diving? maybe

⑰ Would You like to go up IN A HOT AIR BALLOON? yes

⑱ Would you like to RIDE AN ELEPHANT? yes

⑲ Would You like to EXPLORE A CAVE? Yes

⑳ Would You Go on A TREASURE Hunt? yes

㉑ Would You like to stop ANSWERING QUESTIONS ABOUT What You MIGHT WANT To Do? sure

22) WHAT GRADE IN SCHOOL ARE YOU IN ? 6th ✓

23) How much homework Do you Get? NOT MUCH ___✓ ALOT ___ TONS ___

24) What subject Gives you the Most Homework? ___Math___

25) What subject AT SCHOOL is the HARDEST? ___Health___

26) Which is EASY? English, Spelling

27) Is your SCHOOL Too FAR to WALK to? Yes

28) How do you think your grades ARE? NOT Good ___ FAIR ___ Good ___ GREAT ✓

29) Do you liKe YOUR TEACHERS? Yes

30) Is there one you hate? If YES, who

31) WHAT IS SAMSTERS FAVORITE SUBJECT? Reading (He hates science Sometimes his cousins are wise)

32) Which is Best? HOT DOG ___✓ HAMBURGER ___

33) Which is Best? CAKE ___✓ PIE ___

34) Which is Best? CAPTAIN CRUNCH ___✓ CORN FLAKES ___

35) Which is Best? RocK n' Roll ___ RAP ___

36) WHICH IS Best? LIGHTENING ___✓ THUNDER ___

37) WHICH is Best? MOVIES ___✓ TV ___ RADIO ___ RECORDS ___

38) If ANYONE EVER REALLY HURT You OR DiD Something BAD
   To you, WOULD YOU TELL YOUR DAD? YES ___✓ No ___ Don't KNOW ___

39) WHAT is your FAVORITE DINOSAUR? ~~Bront~~ Brontosaurous ~~Tyranosaurus rex~~

40) WHAT IS the WORST INSECT? Wasp

41) WHAT IS the BEST INSECT? ladybug

42) DRAW the WORST INSECT   43) DRAW the BEST INSECT

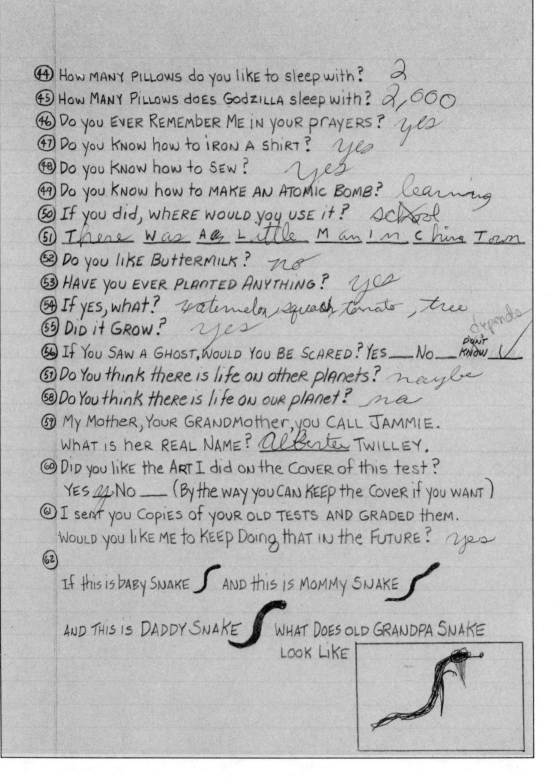

44 How MANY PILLOWS do you like to sleep with? 2

45 How MANY PILLOWS does Godzilla sleep with? 2,000

46 Do you EVER REMEMBER ME IN your prayers? yes

47 Do you KNOW how to IRON A SHIRT? yes

48 Do you KNOW how to SEW? yes

49 Do you KNOW how to MAKE AN ATOMIC BOMB? learning

50 If you did, WHERE WOULD you USE it? school

51 There Was A Little Man In ching Town

52 Do you LIKE BUTTERMILK? no

53 HAVE YOU EVER PLANTED ANYTHING? yes

54 If yes, what? watermelon, squash, tomato, tree

55 DID it GROW? yes

56 If You SAW A GHOST, WOULD YOU BE SCARED? YES ___ No ___ DON'T KNOW ✓ depends

57 Do You think there is life on other planets? maybe

58 Do You think there is life on our planet? na

59 My Mother, Your GRANDMOTHER, you CALL JAMMIE. WHAT IS HER REAL NAME? Alberta TWILLEY.

60 DID you like the ART I did on the COVER of this test? YES ✓ No ___ (By the way you CAN KEEP the COVER if you WANT)

61 I sent you COPIES of YOUR OLD TESTS AND GRADED them. WOULD you like ME to KEEP DOING that IN the FUTURE? yes

62

If this is baby SNAKE ∫ AND this is MOMMY SNAKE ∫

AND THIS is DADDY SNAKE ∫ WHAT DOES OLD GRANDPA SNAKE LOOK LIKE

63 I KNOW you KNOW the 800 Number that you CAN USE to CALL ME FOR FREE. BUT IN CASE OF AN EMERGENCY, Do you KNOW my HOME NUMBER? AREA CODE ____ ____ _____

64 Do you help your MOM AROUND the House?
     YES ✓ No____ ALITTLE ✓ ALOT____

65 NAME SOME WILD ANIMALS you HAVE SEEN SINCE YOU MOVED TO ARKANSAS. *Deer, fox, armidillo, opposum, hawk,*

66 YOUR DAD WAS BORN ON the ____ DAy of the ____ Month AT ____ O'CLOCK AND THE THERE ARE _18_ Letters IN His NAME.

67 WHAT IS the BEST DISNEY MOVIE? *hardone aeah Little Mermaid Anne of Green Gables*

68 Complete the Squiggle.

you complete

Dwight mur Twilley

69 WHAT DID you do with the MARBLES I got you? *kept them for looks*

70 ON AN OLD TEST you SAID you HATED Boys. Do you still? *yes*

71 DID you GET ANY DREADED Socks for X-MAS? *no*

72 Why WOULD you NEVER WANT To Go to NEW YORK? *To dangerous and weird*

73 You should NEVER EAT ANything thats bigger than YOUR HEAD.   TRUE ✓ FALSE _____

74) HAVE you seen "hook" yet? *yes*

75) WOULD you like it if I WROTE A REAL book About the DAD'S TESTS? It COULD help other DAD'S who live FAR AWAY FROM their Kids, MAKE their OWN TESTS. YES _y_ No ___

76) COULD WE GET FAMOUS FOR it? YES _y_ No___ MAYBE ____

77) If I made this book, I WOULD USE PICTURES of you AND ME, AND SHOW the TESTS. WOULD it Bother you if thousands of people saw your drawings AND ANSWERS? YES____ No _y_

78) WOULDN'T it BE funny If Suddenly everyone was CALLING EACH other DADDY, MOMMY or BABY SNAKE, SINGING LITTLE MAN IN CHINA TOWN AND getting letters from their pets. *yes*

79) I WAS SURPRISED you COULDN'T think of A NAME of AN X-MAS SONG I COULD WRITE. CAN you think of A NAME OF ANY KIND of SONG, I COULD WRITE? *? I don't know firefly ?*

80) DRAW,

SUPER TOBY AND BATBUD

81) COULD this MAKE A Good MOVIE? *yes*

82) MOW WANTS to WRITE A letter to PRINCESS. WOULD that BE ok? *yes*

83) Where is the third largest statue of Julio MANGLES IN the WORLD located? *Tulsa*

84 Complete the DRAWING

85 Connect The Dots By Number (You Might Use A Ruler)

86) What is your Favorite part of Julio Mangles? *me ! HA*

87) Is there anything Good About Liver? *well makes a mice*

88) Do you think My printing is good? *yes*

89) Do you think my painting is good? *no* *child*

91) What makes your funny bone funny? *its ticklish* *repelent*

92) Can you Guess how long it took me to make this test? *no*

93) Draw Tanooki Mario

94) Have you ever heard of "ultraman"? *no*

95) Who do you like best, Captain Kirk ___✓___ or Captain Picard _____

96) Who do you like best, Mr Spock ___✓___ or Data _____

97) About How long did it take you to finish this test? _____

98) Could you Call Me Sometime Soon? *yes*

99) Did you think the Grades I gave you on *your* tests were Fair? *yes*

100) Do you Miss Me? *yes*

THE DAD'S TEST FOR DION'S TRIP TO CALIFORNIA, 1992

This special test boasts over 200 exciting questions—and a few stupid ones!

I initiated my "symbol-in-the-box" technique for the simple purpose of deciding what I could feed my kid for two weeks without invoking the dreaded "liver" response! Besides, fourteen pizzas might get a little boring. It also provided me with an interesting overall look at my daughter's diet. I think *"beans and lizards"* and *"rubber pickles"* helped avoid monotony.

The test is divided into Parts I and II. I can't explain the purpose this may have served, but it looked cool!

Subtle aspects of your child's answers may go unnoticed. Only recently I made the following observation. At the beginning of Part II, I listed a succession of twenty yes/no/maybe inquiries. I can see now that the confining regimen here was obviously limiting Dion's capacity to express her answers, and that she had devised a unique solution to the problem. What I once interpreted to be sloppiness or disinterest, was really much more! Dion had used the size and shape of her check marks to demonstrate her emotional response to the questions. When it comes to the "Dad's Tests," expect the unexpected.

QUESTIONS, QUIRKS AND COMMENTS

QUESTION 6 and 7 Earlier, when I mentioned my numbering mistake in test number one, I had no idea of the scope of my almost dyslexic approach to mathematics. Throughout my tests, I find numbers omitted, repeated and placed out of order for no apparent reason. I don't know whether to consult my accountant or see a therapist!

QUESTION 151 *"Which is best: doughnuts or cinnamon rolls?"* Her answer: *"A mystery of the world."* The answer really shows Dion's sense of humor!

QUESTION 153 *"What kind of pipe tobacco do you use?"* An important question that every dad needs to know before a visit of this type.

THE DAD'S TEST FOR DION'S TRIP TO CALIFORNIA 1992

MAY

OVER 200 EXCITING QUESTIONS / AND A FEW STUPID ONES

In the first part of the Test, choose ONE of these FIVE symbols that best describes How You Feel About the items listed.

[♡] LOVE IT

[☺] LIKE IT

[✓] IT'S OK

[☒] HATE IT

[?] DON'T KNOW

I LEFT A SPACE UNDER EACH ITEM, IN CASE YOU HAVE ANY COMMENTS

① Milk [☺] ② Chocolate Milk [☺] ③ Butter Milk [☒]

I like milk alot

④ Apple Juice [♡] ⑤ Orange Juice [☺] ⑥ Prune Juice [☒]

Well actually I've never tried it but...

⑦ Tomato Juice [☒] ⑥ Onion Juice [☒] ⑦ Lemonade [✓]

♡ = LOVE   ☺ = LIKE   ✓ = OK   ✗ = HATE   ? = DON'T KNOW

⑧ CRANAPPLE JUICE [?]   ⑨ ICED TEA [☺]   ⑩ COKE [♡]

⑪ DR PEPPER [♡]   ⑫ 7UP [♡]   ⑬ ROOT BEER [☺]   ⑭ MALTS [?]

⑮ MILK SHAKES [♡]   ⑯ MOTOR OIL [✗]   ⑰ CORN [♡]

accually makes a nice afternoon snack

⑱ CORN ON the COB [♡]   ⑲ CREAM CORN [♡]   ⑳ POP CORN [♡]

㉑ GREEN BEANS [✗]   ㉒ PORK AND BEANS [✗]   ㉓ PEAS [☺]

→ *Only 2 kings* Sweat green ← field purple hull

㉔ BEANS AND WEENIES [✗]   ㉕ BEANS AND LIZZARDS [✗]   ㉖ RICE [✓]

㉗ SPINACH [✗]   ㉘ TOMATOES [✓]   ㉙ BEETS [?]   ㉚ CARROTS [✓]

㉛ LETTUCE [☺]   ㉜ ONION [✗]   ㉝ ASPARAGUS [✗]   ㉞ SQUASH [✗]

㉟ SAUERKRAUT [?]   ㊱ BROCCOLI [✗]   ㊲ CELERY [✓]   ㊳ SPIDERS [✗]

㊴ ARTICHOKES [?]   ㊵ BRUSSELS SPROUTS [✗]   ㊶ MUSHROOMS [?]

㊷ SWEET PICKLES [♡]   ㊸ DILL PICKLES [✗]   ㊹ RUBBER PICKLES [✗]

㊺ GREEN OLIVES [✗]   ㊻ RIPE OLIVES [✗]   ㊼ MASHED POTATOES [♡]

㊽ SWEET POTATOES [?]   ㊾ MR. POTATOE HEAD [✗]   ㊿ PEARS [♡]

51 STRAWBERRIES [♡]   52 BANANNAS [✓]   53 APPLES [✓]   54 ORANGES [☺]

55 PEACHES [♡]   56 BLACKBERRIES [♡]   57 CHERRIES [♡]   58 RAISINS [✗]

♡ = LOVE ☺ = LIKE ✓ = OK X = HATE ? = DONT KNOW

59) PINEAPPLE [♡] 60) GRAPEFRUIT [♡] 61) GRAPES [♡] 62) COCONUT [?]

63) WATERMELON [♡] 64) CANTALOUPE [♡] 65) APRICOTS [♡] 66) LIVER [X]

67) STEAK [♡] 68) HAM [☺] 69) FRIED RAT [♡] 70) PORK CHOPS [♡]

a favorite

71) BACON [♡] 72) SAUSAGE [?] 73) BAKED CHICKEN [♡] 74) TUNA [X]

75) FRIED CHICKEN [♡] 76) FROZEN CHICKEN [X] 77) CHICKEN FRIED STEAK [♡]

78) PEPPERONI [♡] 79) MEAT LOAF [X] 80) MEATBALLS [♡]

81) MEAT NEW FRIENDS [♡] 82) OYSTERS [X] 83) LOBSTER [?] 84) CLAMS [X]

85) SQUID [?] 86) CATFISH [♡] 87) DOG FISH [?] 88) RED SNAPPER [?]

never tried

89) SHRIMP COCKTAIL [?] 90) SHRIMP SCAMPI [?] 91) FRIED SHRIMP [♡]

92) SCRAMBLED EGGS [♡] 93) EGGS SUNNYSIDE UP [?] 94) DEVILED EGGS [?]

95) EGG NOG [X] 96) FROG EGGS [X] 97) OMELETS [?] 98) YOGURT [☺]

99) SALAD [☺] 100) BLUE CHEESE DRESSING [X] THOUSAND ISLAND DRESSING [✓]

102) ITALIAN DRESSING [X] 103) HAIR DRESSING [X] 104) MUSTARD [X]

105) MAYONNAISE [X] 106) MIRACLE WHIP [X] 107) A1 STEAK SAUCE [?]

108) PICKLE RELISH [X] 109) TARTAR SAUCE [X] 110) RANCH DRESSING [♡]

♥=LOVE ☺=LIKE ✓=OK X=HATE ?=DON'T KNOW

(111) SWISS CHEESE [♥]   JACK CHEESE [?]   (113) STRING CHEESE [?]

(114) CREAM CHEESE [♡]   (115) BAGELS [♥]   (116) COTTAGE CHEESE [?]

(117) PARMESAN [?]   (118) SNAILS [X]   (119) SALSA [X]   (120) BAGWORMS [X]

(121) SPAGHETTI [☺]   (122) SPAGHETTI AND CHILLI [✓]   (123) MEATBALLS [1]

(124) MEATBATS [♡]   (125) RITZ CRACKERS [♡]   (126) SALTINE CRACKERS [♡]

(127) FIRE CRACKERS [♥]   (128) GUACAMOLE DIP [X]   (130) BEAN DIP [X]

(131) KITTY LITTER DIP [X]   (132) CHINESE FOOD [✓]   (133) INDIAN FOOD [X]

(134) FRENCH ONION SOUP [?]   (135) STEAK AND BEARNAISE SAUCE [?]

(136) GREEN BEAN AND CHEESE SAUCE [X]   (137) CAESAR SALAD [?]

(138) GARLIC BREAD [♡]   (139) STIR FRY [?]   (140) POTATOE SALAD [?]

(141) NAME YOUR THREE FAVORITE BREAKFAST CEREALS
   ① Captain Crunch Cereal PButter ~~donut~~
   ② Basic 4
   ③ plenty others

(142) WHAT IS YOUR FAVORITE KIND OF COOKIE? <u>Choc. chip</u> pecan
(143) WHAT IS YOUR FAVORITE KIND OF CAKE? <u>vanilla or choc</u>
(144) WHAT IS YOUR FAVORITE KIND OF PIE? <u>cheesecake or peach</u>
(145) WHAT IS YOUR FAVORITE KIND OF SOUP? <u>chicken noodle</u>

(146) What is your FAVORITE FLAVOR ICE CREAM? *choclate*

(147) What is your FAVORITE Pudding? *banana to here*

(148) What is your FAVORITE Poisonous SNAKE? *Rattler*

(149) What is your FAVORITE KIND of chips? *Dirtychips Lays*

(150) Whats on your FAVORITE SANDWICH? *Grill Cheese*

(151) Which is best, DONUTS OR CINNAMON ROLLS? *a mystery of the world*

(152) WHAT Toppings Do you like ON PIZZA? *cheese or hamburger or pepperoni*

(153) WHAT KIND of Pipe Tobacco Do you use? *many kinds*

(154) Which do you like best, bubble BATH OR SHOWER? *shower*

(155) CAN you believe I CAME up with this MANY QUESTIONS? *yep*

(156) Do you hAVE any NEW Photos you Could SEND ME? *yep*

(157) Will you Remember to bring GUM to CHEW on the PLANE? *yep*

(158) ARE you NERVOUS ABOUT flying ALONE? *none*

(160) Who WAS A little MAN INdeed? *A little man in China*

(161) What did the baby SNAKE SAY to the Mommie snake? *s.s.s.ss*
ANSWER: Nothing, SNAKES CAN'T TALK.

(162) Do you think this test is too long? *nope*

(163) Do you promise NOT TO Put COLD DR. Pepper GLASSES ON DAD'S FOOT IN the Morning? *yep*

(164) Does DAD Promise NOT TO hide IN DARK CORNERS, AND MAKE SCARY NoISES? *I dont know*

(165) Will you bring the VIDEO of your pets, So I CAN MAKE A COPY? *Yep and your fathers and b-day preset*

(166) ARE you Going to bring Sunglasses to SUNNY CALIfORNIA? *yep*

(167) Do you think JULIO MANGLES MAY hAVE EVER VISITED DisneylAND? *yep*

(168) Do you think the MONORAIL MAY ONCE hAVE bEEN CALLED — the MANGLESORAIL? *yes he donated it*

(168) What will our Feet feel like when we leave DISNEYLAND? *ows*

(170) Where IN DisneylAND Will DAD WANT TO Go EAT chilli? *crepeloes*
none crepeloes

PART 2

THINGS WE MIGHT WANT TO DO DURING YOUR VISIT. *have fun*

① Go to DISNEYLAND.   YES ✓ No ____ Maybe ____

② ASK EVERYONE AT DISNEYLAND to OUR HOUSE FOR HAMBURGERS.
                        YES ____ No ✓ Maybe ____

③ PLAY VIDEO GAMES.   YES ✓ No ____ Maybe ____

④ MAKE A MOVIE   YES ✓ No ____ Maybe ____

⑤ SET Buildings ON FIRE AND LOOT STORES.
                        YES ✓ No ____ Maybe ____   *Nice Holsom Family Fun*

⑥ Try to keep the puppy out of the pool.
                        YES ✓ No ____ Maybe ____

⑦ Look AT DAD's Collections. YES ✓ No ____ Maybe ____

⑧ HAVE A Robot SHOW.   YES ✓ No ____ Maybe ____

⑨ EAT BARBECUE EVERY NIGHT.
                        YES ____ No ____ Maybe ____

⑩ RECORD A SONG Together IN DAD's studio.
                        YES ____ No ____ Maybe ✓

⑪ HAVE DAD's Photographer Do A PHOTO SESSION of US.
                        YES ____ No ____ Maybe ✓

⑫ WATCH OUR MOVIES, Like Super Dion.
                        YES ✓ No ____ Maybe ____

⑬ Go to Hollywood AND look FOR TRADING CARDS.
                        YES ✓ No ____ Maybe ____

⑭ Dion Works In the Yard All day while DAD Relaxes by the Pool.
          YES ____ No __✓__ Maybe ____

⑮ Drive to the Ocean.
          YES ____ No ____ Maybe _____

⑯ Go to Hollywood And See A Movie IN A Big THEATRE.
          YES __✓__ No ____ Maybe _____

⑰ Go to A DRIVE-IN THEATRE
          YES __✓__ No ____ Maybe _____

⑱ WALK to the PARK AND feed the ducks.
          YES __✓__ No ____ Maybe _____

⑲ TRy FoR Hours to Feed the CeRAmic Duck in my bAckyARD.
          YES ____ No __✓__ Maybe _____

⑳ While We're busy Trying to do All these things, try to hAVE FUN.
          YES __✓__ No ____ Maybe _____

㉑ List Which VIDEO GAMES you ARE Going to bring with you?
    Monster Party
    Majic Kingdom
    Super-land
    Tetris
     Antisipation

㉒ Will you MIND If CARRie WANts To sleep with you? _Nope_

㉓ SINCE SCHOOL will be OUT AND it will be youR VACATION,
  ABOUT WHAT TIME Do you Think you Will WANT To go
  to BED AT NIGHT? ___ 1:00 nothing (HA)___

㉔ What TIME will you get up? ___8:00 or so___

㉕ SINCE the puppy Will AttAck AND kill your stuffed Animals
  I thought I would just put SOME of them in your Room.
  Is that OK? ___ yes ___

26 DRAW MOW AND PRIN SHARING A PIZZA

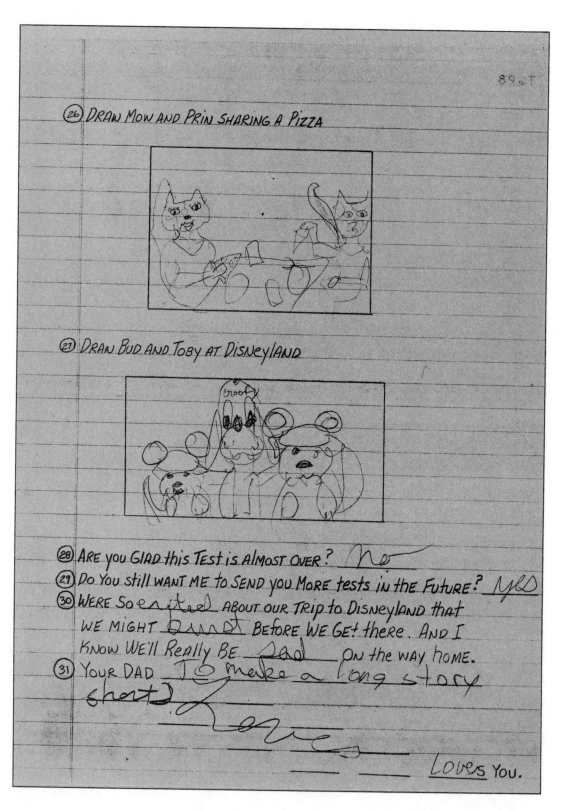

27 DRAW BUD AND TOBY AT DISNEYLAND

28 ARE YOU GLAD this TEST is ALMOST OVER? _No_

29 Do You still WANT ME to SEND you MORE tests in the FUTURE? _Yes_

30 WERE SO _excited_ ABOUT OUR TRIP to DISNEYLAND that
WE MIGHT _arrest_ BEFORE WE GET there. AND I
KNOW WE'll REALLY BE _sad_ ON the WAY HOME.

31 YOUR DAD _To make a long story_
short) _Love's_ YOU.

100 Questions From Dad:
An Extra Excellent
Xmas Examination

W hile I must admit it was really hard coming up with 100 questions about Christmas, it was well worth the effort.

It was great to get a look at how the Snake and Flea families spent Christmas. Toby Claus and Rudolph the Red Nosed Mallard deserve honorable mention as well!

I also introduced some new activities—a "Where's Waldo"-type "Where's Santa," and a "fill-in-the-blank story." Furthermore, the test features the birth of a new, all-purpose holiday, *"The Fourth of Chrisoween-thankseaster Day."* Coming up with these ideas is kind of like throwing darts at a map. You either end up in Beverly Hills—or Death Valley!

It was interesting to learn that Dion would like a pet skunk. Boy, would that be a holiday surprise for the folks back home!

QUESTIONS, QUIRKS AND COMMENTS

QUESTION 38 While really stretching to come up with all these Christmas questions, I came up with this silly query. *"Why does Noel have an 'L' in it?"* I thought her answer was really clever: *"I don't noe."*

QUESTION 39 *"Can you think of a New Year's resolution for 1993?"* She issued the following pledge: *"I won't eat anything with sugar in it . . . NOT!"* A "most excellent" answer, babe!

QUESTION 39 *"Since you couldn't come out for Christmas, do you think maybe you might like a little longer visit this summer—say three or four weeks?"* Sometimes the temptation arises to dream out loud. Try not to ask for decisions that are not your child's to make.

QUESTION 90 Here, I ask Dion to complete my list of *"The ten things you would never want to find under your Xmas tree on Xmas morning."* Her entries:

 6 A dead frog
 7 Rotten apple
 8 A dead Santa
 9 A broken Christmas ornament
10 Nothing

I guess 8 and 10 could throw a wrench in the whole yuletide thing!

① WHAT IS YOUR FAVORITE X-MAS SONG? *White Christmas Silent Night*

② IS THERE A X-MAS SONG you hate? *No*

③ HAVE SUGAR-PLUMS EVER DANCED ON your head? *Yes*

④ I'VE BEEN HAVING fun with ZELDA. WOULD you like it? *Yes*

⑤ IS there ANOTHER VIDEO GAME you Might like?
S. Mario Land Gameboy - any other games?

⑥ ARE YOU GOING to have A X-MAS TREE this YEAR? *Yes*

⑦ NAME three things you WOULD NEVER HANG ON A X-MAS TREE.
   ① *Skunk air freshner*
   ② *raw meat*
   ③ *Prinses*

⑧ How MANY different KINDS of TRADING CARDS do you have now? *zillion*

⑨ Do you KNOW Where you will SPEND X-MAS DAY? *Here probly*

⑩ NAME three BIG things you Might WANT FOR X-MAS.
   ① *TABOO*
   ② *Camera*
   ③ *Electronic Battleship*

⑪ DRAW RUDOLPH THE RED NOSED MALLARD.

⑫ HAVE YOU SAVED SOME MONEY FOR X-MAS PRESENTS? *Yes*

⑬ BESIDES YOUR MOM, WHO WILL YOU GET GIFTS FOR?
YOU

⑭ ARE YOU GOING TO SEND OUT ANY X-MAS CARDS? *Yes*

⑮ WHAT IS ONE OF YOUR FAVORITE X-MAS MOVIES?
The Christmas story Home alone 1+2 etc.

⑯ DRAW TOBY CLAUS

⑰ MAN, A TOWN IN LITTLE WAS CHINA THERE....WHAT COULD
this MEAN? *There was a Little man in china town*

⑱ CLYDE the CAMEL has Nothing to Do with X-MAS. TRUE ___ FALSE ✓

⑲ WOULD YOU LIKE ME to VIDEO YOUR X-MAS PRESENTS LIKE
I did LAST YEAR. *Yes*

⑳ NAME three MEDIUM X-MAS PRESENTS YOU MIGHT WANT.
① *Doodle Dome*
② *for Game Boy - Light Boy + Magnifier*
③ *Video Games*

㉑ IS there A DISNEY MOVIE you don't have that you WOULD LIKE?
Beaty + Beast

22 Who Got Run over by a Reindeer? *Grandma*

23 Draw the Snake Family on X-mas Day.

24 If you Could Give every person in the World a present on X-mas, what would it be? *money or happiness*

25 Santa Claus' Favorite X-mas is the bestest *one of all.*

26 Do you still like stuffed Animals? *Yes*

27 Name All the different Kinds of Animals you have had or have as pets. *Parabeet, hanster mouse frog salanander newt fish dog cat ducks goose snake tadpol chicken*

28 Name three Animals you have never had as pets that you would like to have.
① *skunk*
② *mink or ferret*
③ *horse or cow*

(29) _Dionne_'s X-MAS STORY

Dionne WAS A _young_ GIRL WHO LIVED IN A _small_ TOWN CALLED _Mason_. IT WAS ALMOST _twelve_ O'CLOCK AT NIGHT WHEN SHE WAS WOKE UP BY A _faint_ NOISE. IT SOUNDED LIKE SOMETHING WAS _walking_ ON THE ROOF OF HER HOUSE. EVEN HER CAT _Princess_ WAS _stirring_ AND _jumped_ OFF THE BED. HER DOG _Buddy_ WAS _sitting_ IN THE _large_ YARD. SHE _jumped_ OUT OF BED AND _rushed_ TO THE WINDOW TO SEE WHAT WAS HAPPENING. BUT SHE COULD'NT SEE ANYTHING BECAUSE THE _snow_ WAS FALLING SO _thickly_. BUT WHEN SHE _went_ DOWN THE HALL SHE WAS _able_ TO SEE A _faint_ LIGHT COMMING FROM THE KITCHEN. _Quietly_ SHE CREPT UP AND PEAKED IN ' _the_ CRACK OF THE DOOR. WHAT SHE SAW WAS SO _surprising_ SHE NEARLY _fell_. SURE ENOUGH IT WAS OLD _Saint Nick_ HIMSELF, SITTING AT THE TABLE DRINKING SOME _milk_ AND EATING A _cookie_. SHE RUBBED HER EYES AND LOOKED AGAIN, BUT HE WAS GONE. SHE THOUGHT MAYBE IT WAS JUST A _weird_ DREAM. BUT ON HER WAY BACK TO HER ROOM, SHE NOTICED THE SCREEN ON THE FIREPLACE WAS _moved_ AND THERE WAS _ashes_ ALL OVER THE _carpet_. BUT WHEN SHE _ran_ INTO THE LIVING ROOM, SHE WAS _delighted_ TO SEE _tons_ AND _tons_ OF ALL KINDS OF _presents_ AROUND THE _tree_ TREE. SHE _ran_ BACK TO HER ROOM AND _peered_ OUT THE WINDOW. IT WAS STILL TOO _dark_ TO SEE OUT. BUT IN THE DISTANCE, SHE COULD HEAR _jingle_ BELLS AND A _faint_ VOICE CALLING OUT _Merry_ X-_mas_ TO ALL AND TO ALL A _goodnight_.

(30) AREN'T YOU GLAD All the QUESTIONS AREN'T AS long As
the lAST ONE? *yes*

(31) NAME three SMALL things you MIGHT WANT FOR X-MAS.
① *a cards collection or any collection stuff*
② *a small rubber mouse*
③ *a pink 1956 convertable*

(32) Do you hope it SNOWS ON X-MAS? YES ✓ No____ Don't CARE____

(33) Do you hAVE ENOUGH heaters Now to Keep Your House
WARM For the Winter? YES ✓ No____ NOT SURE____

(34) WHAT ARE the NAMES of ALL Your Ducks that have NAMES So FAR?
① *Mohawk* ⑦ *Pokey* ⑬
② *Whirly Birdlove Jr.* ⑧ *Mallory* ⑭
③ *Mel M.* ⑨ ⑮
④ *Dixie Bell* ⑩ ⑯
⑤ *Geoffrey* ⑪ ⑰
⑥ *Blue Eyes* ⑫ ⑱

(35) DRAW Buddy the SNOWMAN.

36) Do you think your getting TOO OLD FOR the DAD's Tests? *No*

37) Which is the BEST X-MAS DINNER?

TURKEY ____

HAM ✓

EiTHER ____

Both ✓

38) Why does NOEL HAVE AN "L" in it? *I don't NOE*

39) CAN you think of A NEW YEARS RESOLUTION FOR 1993?
I won't eat anything with sugen in i + NOT

40) MIRACLE ON 31 th street.

41) Which of YOUR VIDEO GAMES Do you think you have played
the Most? *Videomation - lattey*

42) NAME three tiny things you MIGHT WANT FOR X-MAS.

① *A band-aid*

② *a jack*

③ *a Trampaleme*

43) Wheres SANTA?, CiRCLE with COLOR MARKER

44. NAME FIVE CARTOON CHARACTERS YOU FOUND While
looking FOR SANTA.
① Bullwinkle
② Snoopy
③. Bugs Bunny
④ Pinnochio
⑤ Fred

45. NAME FIVE other CHARACTERS YOU FOUND WHILE Looking FOR SANTA.
① Spock
② Batman
③ Frankienstein
④ E.T.
⑤ Superman

46. Which ARE NOT other NAMES FOR SANTA CLAUS.

SANTA ____		OLD WHITE BEARD ____ ✓
THE RED ZORRO ____ ✓		SAINT NICHOLAS ____
THE FAT CHRISTMAS DUDE ____ ✓		THE BAG MAN ____ ✓
OLD SAINT NICK ____		FATHER CHRISTMAS ____ ✓
THE CLAUSMEISTER ____ ✓		THE CHIMNEY GUY ____ ✓
KRISS KRINKLE ____		NICE BURGLAR ____ ✓

47. Since there ARE CANDY CANES, why don't they have
CANDY WHEEL CHAIRS? Because it gets
way too slickey

48. If you had to GET SOME CLOTHES FOR X-MAS what
WOULD BE the lEAST HORRIBLE? SOCKS ____ SHOES ____ HAT ____
SHIRT ____ UNDERWEAR ____ COAT ____ GIRDLE ____ DRESS ____
SWEATER ____ JEANS ____ BATMAN CAPE ✓ OTHER ____

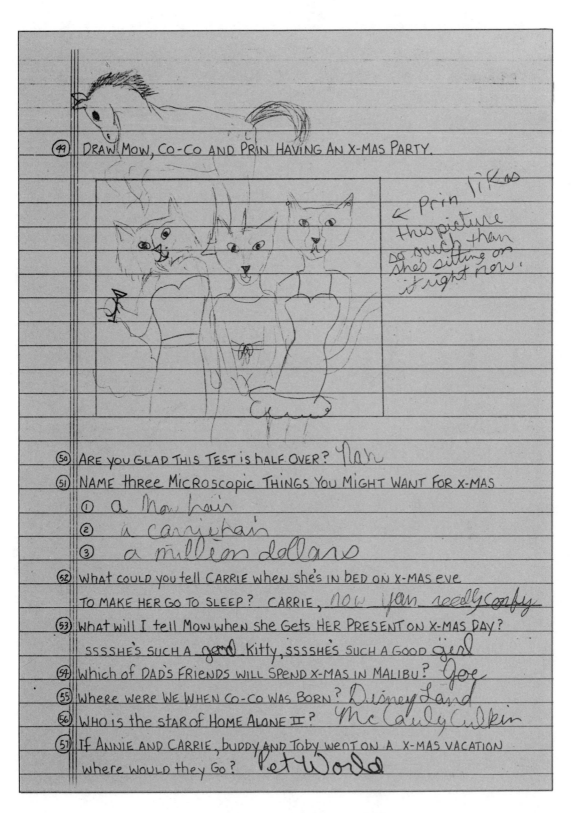

④⑨ DRAW MOW, CO-CO AND PRIN HAVING AN X-MAS PARTY.

← Prin likes this picture so much than she's sitting on it right now.

⑤⓪ ARE YOU GLAD THIS TEST IS HALF OVER? Yah

⑤① NAME three MICROSCOPIC THINGS YOU MIGHT WANT FOR X-MAS

① a Mow hair

② a carrie hair

③ a million dollars

⑤② What COULD you tell CARRIE when she's IN BED ON X-MAS eve TO MAKE HER GO TO SLEEP? CARRIE, now you really confy

⑤③ What will I tell Mow when she Gets HER PRESENT ON X-MAS DAY? SSSSHE'S SUCH A good Kitty, SSSSHE'S SUCH A GOOD girl

⑤④ Which of DAD'S FRIENDS WILL SPEND X-MAS IN MALIBU? Joe

⑤⑤ Where WERE WE WHEN CO-CO WAS BORN? Disney Land

⑤⑥ WHO is the STAR of HOME ALONE II? McCauly Culkin

⑤⑦ If ANNIE AND CARRIE, buddy AND Toby WENT ON A X-MAS VACATION where WOULD they Go? Pet World

(58) DRAW the GHOST of CHRISTMAS PAST

(59) How did the three KINGS FIND the baby JESUS? The star

(60) WHO STOLE CHRISTMAS? The Grinch

(61) I'M DREAMING OF A BLUE CHRISTMAS. TRUE _____ FALSE ✓_____

(62) NAME THREE INVISIBLE things YOU MIGHT WANT FOR X-MAS.

① a mini tree

② a plastic duckset

③ A Mall full of Toys

(63) WHAT is the WORST THING you COULD FIND in your stocking
ON X-MAS MORNING? a lump of coal or a scorpian

(65) what did diNOSAURS USE FOR X-MAS TREES? Bronto bones

(66) WHAT DO ASTRONAUTS Get FOR X-MAS?

Ⓐ MISTLETOE _____

Ⓑ PEACE OFF EARTH _____

Ⓒ A GREAT VIEW of the NORTH POLE ✓_____

Ⓓ OTHER Freeze Dried apple sauce

67. How does Mrs Claus get the dirt and soot out of Santa's suit the day after X-mas?
  Ⓐ with Yule Tide _✓_
  Ⓑ Ivory Snow ____
  Ⓒ Christmas Joy ____
  Ⓓ Other _____

66. Draw the following:

A FLEA

FLEA FAMILY AROUND
THE X-MAS TREE

A FLEA'S X-MAS
STOCKING

FLEA CHRISTMAS PARADE

67. What could Ratina get Mr Rat for X-mas? a sweater

68. Who was the Master Mind behind the Invention of Aluminum X-mas Trees?
  Ⓐ Reynolds Wrapner ____
  Ⓑ Al Loumantree ____
  Ⓒ Julio Mangles _✓_

69. Do you think Elvis is still alive and lives with Santa at the North Pole? Yes

70. Name three thing you would never want for X-mas.
  ① Free cardboard box full of foam chips
  ② fingernail clips
  ③ dust

(71) NAME three X-MAS SONGS YOUR DAD WROTE.

① Christmas love

②

③

(72) TELL HOW WE WOULD SPEND the day AND NIGHT IF CHRISTMAS, HALLOWEEN, THANKSGIVING, the 4th of July AND EASTER WERE ALL ON THE SAME DAY.

"THE 4TH OF CHRISOWEENTHANKSEASTER DAY"

FIRST Thing in the Morning WE Would...

Throw fireworks, open presents, carve the pumpkin, stuff the turky+find the eggs.

Simplified

(73) WHERE DID you have thanksgiving DINNER? Martio

(74) WHAT DID you have? ham

(75) How MANY Days until X-MAS? 20

(76) ARE you excited yet? YES ✓ No ___ NOT YET ___ KINDA ___

(77) CHECK ITEMS YOU MIGHT NOT WANT FOR X-MAS.

① Books ___   ⑦ JEWELERY ___

② LUNCH MEAT ✗   ⑧ LIQUID PLUMBER ✗

③ PUZZLES ___   ⑨ MORE DUCKS ✗

④ CHEWING TOBACCO ✗   ⑩ WEED WACKER ✗

⑤ G.I JOE ✗   ⑪ BOARD GAMES ___

⑥ FOOTBALL HELMET ✗   ⑫ AFRO WIG ___ — every year DAD

78 DRAW YOU AND I HAVING A
4th OF CHRISOWEENTHANKSEASTER DAY PARTY.

79 is there ANother one of your TRADING CARDS you WOULD
Like the FULL SET OF? *MAD—ELVIS etc.*

80 LIST the Things you COLLECT. *Oh gosh, uh—stickers*
pencils, pens, erasers, cards, pets, ducks
geese, duan, etc.

81 WhAt COULD I do to keep FROM BEING SAD SINCE you CAN'T
BE here FOR X-MAS? *eat choclate icecream*

82 IF It SNOWED OVER the Holidays, Would you build A SNOWMAN?
YES ✓ No ___ MAybE ___ SNOWDUCK ✓ SNOWSNAKE ___

83 HAVE you ever builT A SNOWMAN? *Yes*

84. HAVE you ever MAde X-MAS cookies? Yes
85. HAVE you ever MAde FISH ICE CREAM? every year
86. Does it Sound like I'M RUNNING OUT of X-MAS Questions? No
87. WHAT would be A good ideA FOR A Movie FOR us to MAKE THIS SummeR? Another Mr. Rat (Your X-present hint)
88. Since you Couldn't Come out FoR X-MAS, Do you think Maybe you Might like A little longer VISIT this SummeR, SAy THREE OR FOUR Weeks? Maybe
89. Do you think 100 QUESTIONS ARE Too MANY? NA
90. Complete the list of Ten things you would Never WANT To find under youR Tree on X-MAS MORNING.
   ① LIVE RATTLE SNAKE
   ② LAST YEARS X-MAS presents
   ③ twenty GAllons of COLESLAW
   ④ DRACULA'S COFFIN
   ⑤ A BLAZING FIRE
   ⑥ A dead frog
   ⑦ rotten apple
   ⑧ A DEAD SANTA
   ⑨ A broken christmas ornament
   ⑩ NOTHING!!!
91. If I COULD Look IN SANTA'S Book UNDER DioN Twilley IN 1992 it WOULD SAY, She WAS MEAN AND bEAT UP her ducks ____ she WAS ok, but did'nt Try hARD At school ____ she WAS Good but let her FiSH DIE ____ She WAS Just GREAT ____ she WAS perfect IN everyway! ____ she helped SAVE Co-Co's Life, her DAD should SEND her Tons of Presents ✓

92) DRAW the following:

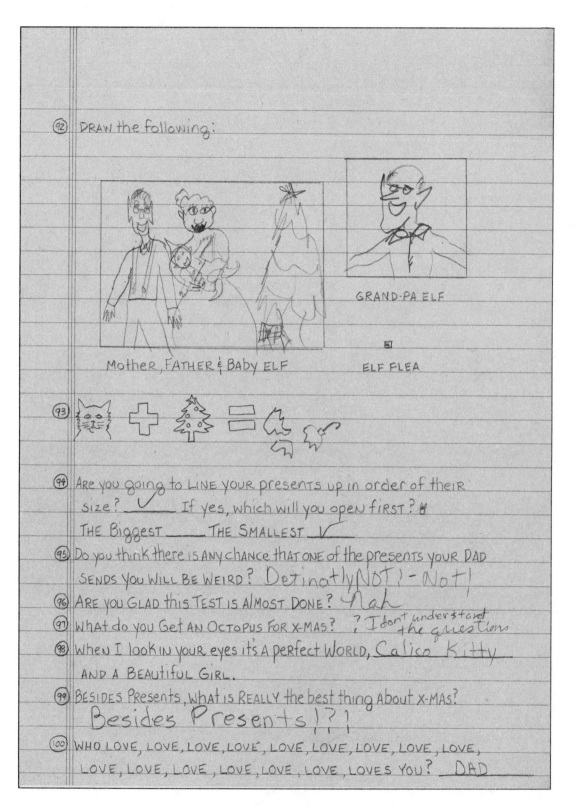

Mother, FATHER & BABY ELF   ELF FLEA   GRAND-PA ELF

93)

94) Are you going to LINE YOUR presents up in order of their
size? ___✓___ If yes, which will you open FIRST?
THE Biggest _____ THE SMALLEST ✓

95) Do you think there is ANY chance THAT ONE of the presents YOUR DAD
SENDS YOU WILL BE WEIRD? Detinotly NOT) - Not!

96) ARE YOU GLAD this TEST IS ALMOST DONE? Nah

97) WHAT do you Get AN OCTOPUS FOR X-MAS? ? I don't understand the questions

98) When I look in your eyes it's A perfect WORLD, Calico Kitty
AND A BEAUTIFUL GiRL.

99) BESIDES Presents, WHAT IS REALLY the best thing About X-MAs?
Besides Presents)?)

100) WHO LOVE, LOVE, LOVE, LOVE, LOVE, LOVE, LOVE, LOVE, LOVE,
LOVE, LOVE, LOVE, LOVE, LOVE, LOVE, LOVE, LOVES YOU? ___DAD___

100 QUESTIONS
FROM DAD 1993

I t's hard to be objective, but it seems like the
tests are improving with age. "Super Flea" and
"The Singing Fish Head" are, for my money, top
notch illustrations. The complete-the-blank-story, *"The
Big Green Rat From Outer Space With Christmas
Lights On Its Tail,"* is an undeniable literary milestone.

This test also includes my first, and hopefully, last
attempt at a crossword puzzle, and a somewhat successful diagram of *"A Day In The Life Of My Daughter
At School."*

Dion and I are aspiring to be the Lennon and
McCartney of "Dad Testing."

QUESTIONS, QUIRKS AND COMMENTS

QUESTION 19 I didn't really know what would happen
when I asked, *"What could squirmeyblobin mean?"*
My scholarly daughter's learned response was
"SQUIRMEYBLOBIN (noun) 1. *The act of having an
unlawful squirmey blob in your house."* I didn't know
that!

QUESTION 24 *"Name something your Dad loves that you hate."* Her answer: *"Cigarettes."* Ouch! I guess she busted me there.

QUESTION 25 I was surprised that when I asked her to *"name something your dad hates that you love,"* she answered, *"Arkansas."* I'll have to let her know that the only thing I hate about Arkansas is the distance it puts between us!

QUESTION 30 *"At what age do you think you'll be too old for the Dad's Test?"* Her answer: *"204, give or take a year."* After all the time I have invested in the Dad's Tests, this one answer alone makes it all worthwhile! Perhaps these questionnaires will, in fact, weather the teenage years, or even a lifetime.

QUESTION 61 With her answer, my daughter lets me know that homework is not really necessary for her. I'm not sure how serious she is, and I suppose that this is an issue to be concerned about. But since Dion consistently earns straight "A's," I figure, why rock the boat by pursuing the matter? Something tells me she might be sneaking in a tiny bit of homework between video games.

① NAME YOUR three FAVORITE BIG things you GOT FOR X-MAS.
  ① Keyboard
  ② My horses -(not real)
  ③ camera
② ARE you GLAD TOBY is home? yes
③ WHAT DID he LOOK like when he RETURNED? Not exacley a Toby form ah...
④ WHAT DO you think he WAS doing? Going to a health clinic
⑤ NAME YOUR three FAVORITE Medium things you GOT FOR X-MAS
  ① Taboo
  ② cards
  ③ Waynes World pin
⑥ DID you have FUN IN Little Rock? yes
⑦ WHAT WAS the Most NOTABLE thing you did there? drive
⑧ DRAW TOBY AFTER RETURNING FROM His Adventure.

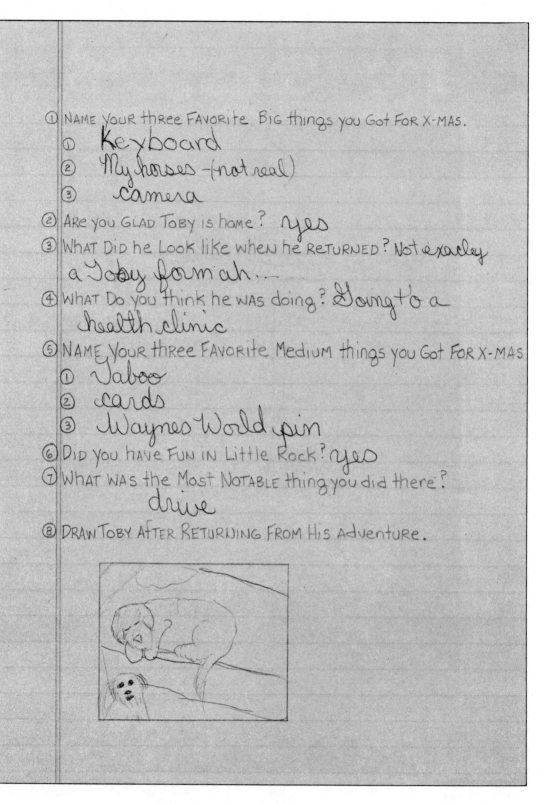

⑨ Did you like my X-Mas Video? *yes*

⑩ When are you Sending me Your X-Mas Video? *soon*

⑪ What was your Favorite thing in my X-Mas Video? *The merry x-mas greetings*

⑫ How will We explain to people what Baby Snakes Are? ~~ ?

⑬ And if You Wonder What the story is *here it is here it is here it is*

⑭ Mark the things you're pretty Sure you would Never Want To Do For A Living.

Tow Truck driver ✓   Bank Robber ✓

Banker ___   Actress ___

Mortician ✓   Artist ___

Lawyer ___   Writer ___

Veterinarian ___   Mechanic ✓

Nurse ✓   Plumber ✓

Singer ___   Cop ✓

Doctor ___   President ___

Scientist ___   Astronaut ___

Chef ✓   Trash Collector ✓

Hairdresser ✓   Psychic ___

Housewife ___   Dentist ✓

⑮ Did I Leave Anything Out? *environmentalist*

16. NAME YOUR three FAVORite SMALL things YOu GoT FOR X-MAS
   ① little iron horse
   ② fire hydrant
   ③ Snowwhite + the seven dwarfs
17. How MANY days tiL X-MAS? about - 2⊄ 265 maybe?
18. DRAW the FOLLOWING:

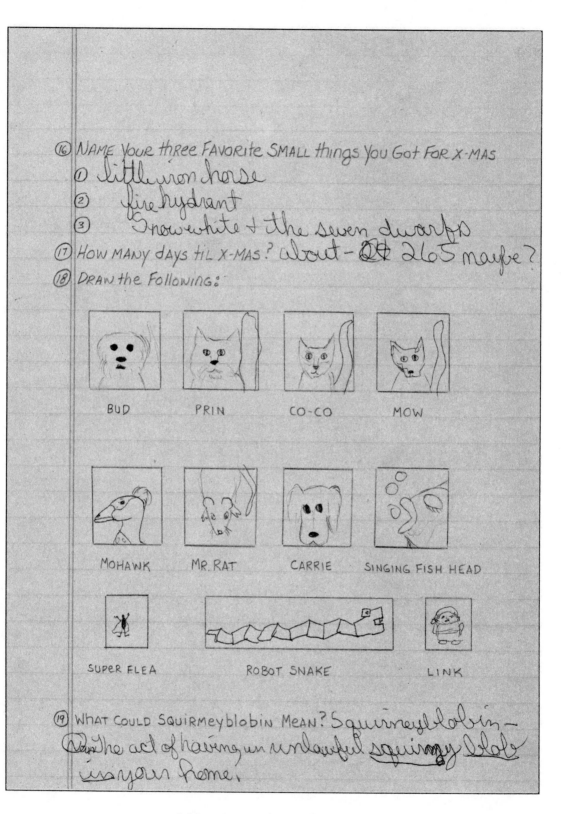

BUD   PRIN   CO-CO   MOW

MOHAWK   MR. RAT   CARRIE   SINGING FISH HEAD

SUPER FLEA   ROBOT SNAKE   LINK

19. WHAT COULD SQUIRMEYBLOBIN MEAN? Squirmeyblobin — the act of having an unlawful squirmy blob in your home.

20) What is the Best thing About your DAD? He's weird + funny!

21) What is the Best thing About you? I'm weird + funny.

22) What is the Worst thing About your DAD? He's weird + funny

23) What is the Worst thing About you? I'm weird + funny

24) NAME Something YOUR DAD Loves that you HATE.
cigarettes

25) NAME Something you Love that YOUR DAD HAtes.
Arkansas?

26) NAME Something WE Both Love. Animals

27) NAME Something WE Both HATE. leeches

28) What is OUR FAVORITE PLACE to Go? Disneyland

29) What is OUR FAVORITE PLACE NOt To Go? in a cardboard box.

30) At WHAt AGE Do you think YOu'll be TOo OLD FOR the DAD'S TESTS?
204 give or take a year

31) At WHAt AGE WILL I bE too OLD to SEND them? 204 give or take a year

32) Do ANy of YOUR fRIENDS Also hAVE DADs that live FAR AWAY?
I dont think so but Kristy Jacksons dad lives in Bryant, Ark.

(33) DAD'S EXCELLENT CROSSWORD PUZZLE... NOT:

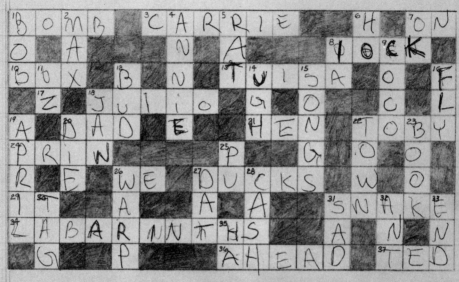

ACROSS

1 ATOMIC _____
3 SHE'S REALLY COMFY
7 IT'S NOT OFF
8 _____ THE DOOR
10 LITTER _____
13 YOU WERE BORN THERE
17 THE MARK OF ZORRO
18 _____ MANGLES
20 HE LOVE LOVE LOVES YOU
21 A FEMALE BIRD
22 ARMADILLO HUNTER
24 A TORTOISE SHELL KITTY
26 THIRD WORD IN QUESTION (26)
27 YOU HAVE TOO MANY
29 _____ CAME FROM OUTER SPACE
31 BABY _____
34 THE TRIFORCES CAN only be found in the
36 FULL SPEED _____
37 BILL AND _____

DOWN

1 WHAT ABOUT _____
2 THIS DOG HAS NO LEGS
4 SHE LIVES IN DOGGIE HEVEN
5 GOES OUT FOR A PIZZA
7-8 6 SANTA SAYS THIS TWICE
↓ 9 MOW'S BABY
11 WHERE TO FIND THE WIZARD
12 HE FOLLOWS TOBY
14 IN THE MOVIES INDAINS SAY it (NOT HOW)
15 DAD WRITES THEM
18 16 THE SPIDER AND the _____
↓ 19 A GOOD MIDDLE NAME
20
↓ 22 CHINA _____
23 THIS TEST COULD END UP IN A _____
25 PEOPLE SAY this when A SKUNK'S AROUND
26 HELPS MARIO GET to Another WORLD
27 OUR INITIALS
28 THE BEST KIND OF MONEY
30 31 NOT HAPPY
↓
32 A BUG THAT COMES TO YOUR PICNIK
33 YOUR NEAR the _____ of this PUZZEL
35 YOU MIGHT SAY THIS WHEN you hear A JOKE

oop's, left these out →
30 YOUR GLAD TOBY WEARS ONE
18 SHE SENT YOU A CAMERA
20 WHAT YOUR FISH DO
7 SHORT FOR OKLAHOMA
8 WHERE DAD LIVES

34) If you hAd Plenty of food But you were left Completely ALONE AT YOUR House FoR A Week it would be

Ⓐ OK _____

Ⓑ Alittle ScARy _____

Ⓒ NIGHT OF THE LIVING DEAD _____ ✗

Ⓓ PARTY TIME ✓_____

35) If you hAd Plenty of Money But you were left Completely ALONE AT the DIsNeyland HOTEL FoR A Week it would be

Ⓐ OK _____

Ⓑ Alittle ScARy _____

Ⓒ "TWILLIGHT" ZONE _____

Ⓓ PARTY TIME ✓_____

36) If you hAd Plenty of RAID But you were left Completely ALONE AT the Bottom of A DARK CAVE With Thousands of BLAck Widow Spiders FoR A Week it would be

Ⓐ Interesting _____

Ⓑ A tAd unsettling _____

Ⓒ AHHHHHH ✓_____

Ⓓ PARTY TIME _____

37) What is the ScARiest thing you CAN Think of ?
Walking down a dark alley at 12:00 am in N.Y.

38) What is the Most Fun thing you could IMAGINE?
Going on a wild animal safari and seeing wild animals

㊴ DRAW YOUR ANSWER to ㊲

㊵ Do YOU READ the NEWSPAPER?
Ⓐ NeveR _____
Ⓑ SoMeTiMeS ✓
Ⓒ EveRY dAY _____
㊶ WhAt is YOUR FAVORite MAGAZINE? Seventeen
㊷ ONe FROZEN DUCK CAN RUiN YOUR WHOLE DAY. TRUE ✓ FALSE _____
㊸ DAD ShOULD Stick to SONgwriting, AND FORget CROSSWORD PUZZLeS.
True _____ FALSE ✓
㊹ YOU WANt to chANge YOUR HAIR to look like CheLSeA Clinton.
True _____ FALSE ✓
㊺ Toby wANts to ChANge his HAIR to look like CheLSeA Clinton.
True _____ FALSE ✓
㊻ PRiN WANts to chANge her hAIR to look like Socks.
True _____ FALSE ✓

47) Do you know Much About Computers? *not really*

48) Would You like one? *yes*

49) What is the strangest Sound Your Casio Makes? *a warbing t laser beam*

50) Are you Glad this Test is half over? *no*

51) *Once There* was a *hairy* Man who
LIVED with his BALDHEADED Dog NAMED *Harry*
and his CROSSEYED CAT, *Bongo* . His *Small*
HOUSE WAS ABOUT *20* MILES FROM the *Small*
TOWN OF *Baldknob*. One *dark* NIGHT JUST
AFTER FINISHING A *full* PLATE OF *Ham*
AND *cheese* AND A little *leg of lamb* FOR
DESSERT, *He* WAS Disturbed by *Harry*
BARKING AT Something Out the *open* WINDOW.
Even *Bongo* Woke up FROM A *cat* NAP
AND STARTED to Make A *scared* Sounding Meow.
He *slowly* Went OUTSIDE to See What WAS the
MATTER. HoLY *fingernail!* He COULD'NT BELIEVE
What he SAW. THERE IN the sky JUST Above him
WAS A HUGE *Rat* with *red* AND
green LIGHTS AND A STRANGE *chittering*
Sound. *Bongo* AND *Harry* WERE SO *scared*
They both *ran* BACK INTO the House AND HID
UNDER the *Bed*. Suddenly it APPEARED THAT

the _Rat_ WAS GOING to _ram_ RIGHT INTO the OLD _Oak_ Tree IN his _front_ YARD. AND Then _Boom_! There WAS A GIANT _explosion_ with _cloudy_ SMOKE AND _orange_ FLAMES. _Harry_ AND _Bob_ SLOWLY _crept_ OUT OF THE House AND ALL _scared_ INTO the SMOKING _mass_ To see if ANYthing WAS left. SURE eNOUGH, There it WAS, A ReAL _Rat_ ABOUT the Size of A _Blue Whale_ in their OWN YARD. They Were So _Scared_ they Were _frozen_. The NEXT day, All the people FROM THE TOWN OF _Baldknob_ CAME to SEE the _crash_ SITE. AS A RESULT _Bob_ BECAME SO _rich_ AND FAMOUS HE WAS Able to buy A Nice Toupee FOR _Harry_ AND SPECIAL GLASSES FOR _Bongo_. It WAS TRULY A _interesting_ experience. BUT They All LIVED _happily_ ever _after_

52) WHAT COULD BE A NAME FOR this STORY? _The big green rat from outer space with christmas lights on its tail_

52) COULD WE MAKE A MOVIE of this STORY? _Sure_

53) QUESTION 51 WAS... HARD _____ EASY _____ FUN ✓ _____ TORTURE _____

54) If OUR story (QUESTION 51) BECAME A BOOK, dRAW what the COVER Would look like.

55) HAVE you ever played A VIDEO GAME CALLED JOURNEY TO SILIUS? no

56) How FAR HAVE you Got with ZELDA? not very far not even to the 2nd labruth

57 How FAR CAN YOU Get in MARIO II ? *About world 5 or 6*

58 Could You Show Me What your SCHEDULE AT SCHOOL IS LIKE?

   (EXAMPLE)

   ENGLISH   X   8:00 Am TIL 9:00 AM

   ★ SCIENCE   10:00 AM TIL 11:00 AM

   LUNCH   11:00 AM TIL 12:00 PM

   (About)

   ^ P.E.   8:15 — 9:00

   X *Geography* 9:10 10:00

   Break ★ *Life Skills, Art (Health)* Music Survey 10:00-11

   Lunch — *English*   11 — 12:00

   ☆ *Life Science* 1:00 — 2:00

   ^ *Math*   1:30 3:45

   ★ *Language Arts (typing)* 2:45 — 3:15

   I have no idea

59 Put A STAR by Your FAVORITE Subjects.

60 PUT A X AFTER Subjects you don't like.

61 ABOUT How Much HOMEWORK Do you usually have ON
   SCHOOL NIGHTS? ½ HOUR ____ HOUR ____ HOUR AND ½ ____
   Never Do Any X Work All Night TIL DAWN ____

62 CAN Ducks SURVIVE with No WATER to SWIM IN ? *Yes
   but they'll get sick a lot*

63) COMPLETE THE DRAWING:

64) DID YOU NOTICE that there were two Questions Number 52 No
65) What does this MEAN? ~~xxxxxxxxxxxxxx~~
  A) This Question Should be 66 ✓
  B) This Test Should be Called 101 Questions FROM DAD ✓
  C) DAD CAN'T COUNT TO 100 ✓
  D) DAD Really Likes the Number 52 ✓
  E) DAD IS LOSING his MIND ✓
  F) ALL OF THE ABOVE ✓
66) HOW MANY VIDEO GAMES DO you have? II Nintendo 5 Gameboy
67) HOW MANY DISNEY MOVIES DO you have? 4

68) What Does Your Room look like?
- Ⓐ NEAT AND CLEAN _____
- Ⓑ NOT TOO BAD _____
- Ⓒ DISASTER AREA ✓_____

69) Do you Think I should
- Ⓐ GROW A MUSTACHE _____
- Ⓑ GROW A BEARD _____
- Ⓒ STAY the SAME ✓_____

70) Which three Questions IN this Test did You like the Best?
- ⑱ Draw the following
- ⑲ What does squirmy labin mean?
- ㉝ Exellent Crossword

71) Check Which things you do pretty Regularly to help Your MOM AROUND the house
- Ⓐ WASH DISHES _____
- Ⓑ VACUUM _____
- Ⓒ SET RAT TRAPS _____
- Ⓓ COOK _____
- Ⓔ TAKE OUT TRASH _____
- Ⓕ BRING IN TRASH _____
- Ⓖ FEED PETS ✓_____
- Ⓗ CHOP DOWN TREES FOR FIREWOOD _____
- Ⓘ DUST _____
- Ⓙ CHANGE FLAT TIRES _____
- Ⓚ DO LAUNDRY _____
- Ⓛ PICK COTTON _____
- Ⓜ SLOP THE HOGS _____
- Ⓝ SET TABLE _____
- Ⓞ MAKE BEDS _____
- Ⓟ LAY IN BED ✓_____
- Ⓠ CREATE EXOTIC FLOWER ARRANGEMENTS _____

72 where's MALLARD?

73 WHAT ANIMAL IS HARD to DRAW? human, frog, moose
74 WHAT ANIMAL IS EASY to DRAW? duck, horse, dog
75 DRAW the ANIMAL you think you do best.

Sitting Duck

76) Who is the funniest CARTOON Character? *Garfield*

77) Do you have ANY PLANS FOR the 4th of CHRISOWEEN THANKS EASTER DAY?
- Ⓐ SAME AS EVERY YEAR _____
- Ⓑ SAVED LAST YEARS eggs FOR under Tree _____
- Ⓒ NOT buying FIREWORKS FOR the turkey this year _____
- Ⓓ TRYING NEW stuffing FOR the PUMPKIN _____
- Ⓔ *Hunting green pumpkins this year* ✓

78) COMPLETE THE SQUIGGLE:

79) SIGN YOUR AUTOGRAPH

Dionne Brulley

80) Do you think you Would ever WANT TO JOIN, the ARMY _____ NAVY _____ AIR FORCE _____ Boy Scouts _____

no

81. DRAW the CO-CO-STEIN MONSTER:

82. CHECK THINGS YOU PLAN TO DO THIS SUMMER:
    A Go SWIMMING ___✓___
    B Get TATOO of SNAKE ON YOUR FOREHEAD _____
    C VISIT DAD ___✓___
    D Go to DisNeyLAND _____
    E Study HeAD HuNTiNG _____
    F MAke ARMADILLO CLOTHes _____
    G Take Pets oN WALks ___✓___
    H Get youR Nose PieRCeD _____

83. Do you think perhaps you MIGHT look NICE with your head shaved AS weLL? Oh I've tried it it's just not me,

84. DRAW You with head shaved AND stylish TATOO AND Nose riNG:

85) If you found a MAGIC LANTERN AND A GENIE APPEARED AND OFFERED YOU ONLY THREE WISHES, What Would THEY BE?

① clean enviroment
② better economy
③ lots of money!

86) Which Would be Good NEW HOLIDAYS?
① NATIONAL NINTENDO DAY ✓
② JULIO MANGLES DAY ✓
③ TOILET CLEANING DAY _____
④ HOT DOG DAY _____
⑤ SLUG DAY _____

87) When the TERMINATOR COMES to YOUR door you should
Ⓐ OFFER HIM COMPUTER CHIPS AND DIP _____
Ⓑ KICK HIM IN the RobUTT _____
Ⓒ DRINK YOUR MAGIC FORMULA BECAUSE you SENSE there MAY be TROUBLE ✓

88) What is YOUR FAVORITE SCARY MOVIE? Shining I think
89) ARE you IN ANY CLUBS AT SCHOOL? Pepclub, QuizBowl
90) Do you think PEOPLE WILL ever stop hAVING WARS? Not really
91) MAYbE they Could have BIG PICNICS INSTEAD TRUE ✓ FALSE _____
92) CAN you Believe this Test is ALMOST OVER? YES _____ No ✓
No LONGER CAPABLE OF THINKING _____

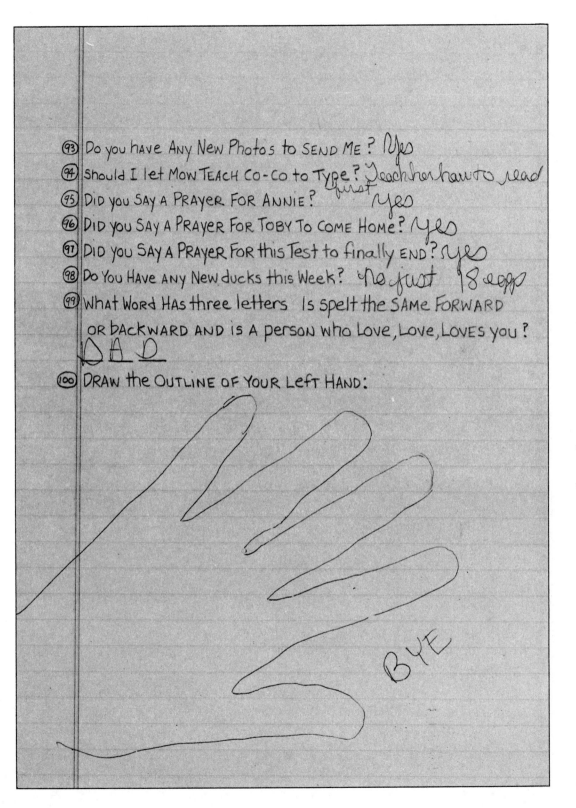

93 Do you have Any New Photos to SEND ME? Yes

94 Should I let Mow TEACH Co-Co to Type? Teach her how to read first

95 Did you SAY A PRAYER FOR ANNIE? Yes

96 DID you SAY A PRAYER FOR TOBY To COME Home? Yes

97 DID you SAY A PRAYER FOR this Test to finally END? Yes

98 Do You HAVE ANY New ducks this Week? No just 18 eggs

99 What Word HAS three letters Is spelt the SAME FORWARD

OR bACKWARD AND iS A person who Love, Love, LOVES you?

DAD

100 DRAW the OUTLINE OF YOUR Left HAND:

BYE

DAD AND DIONNE'S ART GALLERY

◀ • • • • •

"Old Friends,"
by Dwight

"Duck in Sunday Best,"
by Dionne

"Dinos Dining,"
by Dionne

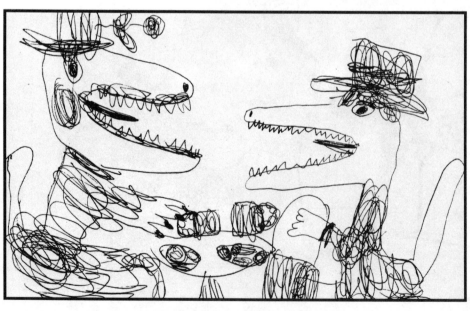

"He's Not From My Side of the Family,"
by Dwight

"Super Toby and Bat Bud,"
by Dionne

"Stone Face," by Dwight

• • • • • • • • • • • • ▶

◀ • • • • • • • • • • • • •

"Mickey Mouse,"
by Dionne

An Open Letter to Other Dads

Dear Dads,

I hope that you have as much fun and success with your Dad's Test as I have.

As I near completion of this book, I am pleased to report that things are going well for Dion and me today. Dion is happy living with her mom in Arkansas, and I like the idea of her growing up where concrete obstacles don't block her view of the sky. As for me, I think that the old man upstairs has taken more than good care! Dion and I see each other as much as possible; we yak on the phone and exchange some letters. But the "Dad's Tests" are still our most "dad-daughterly" means of conversation.

I'm sure that, during the course of receiving the completed tests from your child, you will find answers and artwork that are sometimes profound, heartwarming or hilarious.

I would greatly appreciate your sending me copies of some of your favorite tests, answers or artwork—especially those which defy description!

I would also be very interested in your comments, tips or any new techniques that you have found to be successful. Please feel free to write me in care of my publisher.

I am eagerly looking forward to your correspondences!

Sincerely,

DWIGHT TWILLEY

> **"**
> The Dad's Tests are still the most dad-daughterly means of conversation.
> **"**

FRIENDS AND
SYMPATHETIC EARS

Contact these organizations for information or complete lists of state and local chapters and affiliates. Many organizations distribute monthly or quarterly newsletters containing a great deal of useful information. Computer users with modems can access information directly from the National Congress of Men and Children's Bulletin Board (BBS) (602) 840–4752 or (913) 432–1163.

CHILDREN'S RIGHTS COUNCIL
220 "I" Street, NE #230
Washington, D.C. 20002–4362
(202) 547–6227

AMERICAN ASSOCIATION FOR MARRIAGE AND
FAMILY THERAPY
1100 Seventeenth Street, NE 10th Floor
Washington D.C. 20036
(202) 452–0109

NATIONAL CONGRESS OF MEN AND CHILDREN
2020 Pennsylvania Avenue, NW #277
Washington, D.C. 20006
(800) 773–DADS

ACADEMY OF FAMILY MEDIATORS
1500 South Highway 100, #355
Golden Valley, MN 55416
(612) 525–8670

FATHERS FOR EQUAL RIGHTS, INC.
3623 Douglas Avenue
Des Moines, IA 50310–5345
(515) 277–8789

CHILD WELFARE LEAGUE OF AMERICA
440 First Street, NW #310
Washington, D.C. 20001–2085
(202) 638–2952

MOTHERS WITHOUT CUSTODY
P.O. Box 27418
Houston, TX 77227–7418
(800) 457–MWOC

COALITION FOR AMERICA'S CHILDREN
1634 "I" Street, NW 12th Floor
Washington, D.C. 20006
(202) 638–5770

NATIONAL COALITION OF FREE MEN
P.O. Box 129
Manhasset, NY 11030
(516) 482–6378

FAMILY RESOURCE COALITION
200 South Michigan Avenue, #1520
Chicago, IL 60604
(312) 341–0900

NATIONAL ASSOCIATION OF STATE VOCAL
ORGANIZATIONS
P.O. Box 621314
Orangevale, CA 95662–1314
(800) 745–8778

NATIONAL INSTITUTE FOR RESPONSIBLE
FATHERHOOD AND FAMILY DEVELOPMENT
8555 Hough Avenue
Cleveland, OH 44106
(216) 791–1468

STEPFAMILY ASSOCIATION OF AMERICA
215 Centennial Mall South, #212
Lincoln, NE 68508
(402) 477–7837

GRANDPARENTS UNITED FOR CHILDREN'S RIGHTS
137 Larkin Street
Madison, WI 53705
(608) 238–8751

PARENTS WITHOUT PARTNERS, INTERNATIONAL
401 North Michigan Avenue
Chicago, IL 60611–4267
(312) 644–6610

ABOUT THE AUTHOR

Photo by Robert Knight

D wight Twilley is a writer and rock music artist of international repute. Best known for his hits "I'm on Fire" and "Girls," he has released numerous albums on the Shelter, Arista, EMI and DCC record labels.

A native of Tulsa, Oklahoma, Dwight began painting and writing poetry at a young age. His musical career began at age fifteen, when he found his brother's abandoned guitar in a closet: Dwight was enthralled to find that his words and images could take on new meaning by being fused with melodies.

In 1974, Dwight met drummer and singer Phil Seymour, and together they formed the Dwight Twilley Band. After being signed by Shelter Records, the first song they recorded, "I'm On Fire," was an instant smash. The band's debut album, *Sincerely*, was named "Debut Album of the Year" by *Rolling Stone* magazine.

During the eighties, Dwight and his band toured the world with Jefferson Starship, The Edgar Winter Group, and Greg Kihn. He performed at the 1984 summer Olympics and played for the troops of Desert Storm on the aircraft carrier USS Ranger in 1991. He has been a presenter at the American Music Awards, and had his own hour-long special on MTV. His music has been featured in such films as *Heavenly Bodies, Up the Academy, Just One of the Guys, Worth Winning, Ladybugs,* and *Wayne's World.*

Dwight has never lost his interest in the visual arts, and in 1982 his original works were exhibited in a one-man show at the Museum of Rock Art in Los Angeles. His artistic and literary endeavors have come full circle in the questionnaires he creates for his daughter Dionne. Through them, Dwight reveals the full range of his powers of self-expression.